Advance Praise for

Unstuck & Renewed

"*Unstuck and Renewed* at its core invites you on a journey of discovery in reconnecting with yourself. When we better understand and hold space for each season's energies, we become more aware of our own. This book provides a foundation to explore who we are and the work that is truly a prerequisite for healing and growth."

— *ASHLEY BEAVERSON*

UNSTUCK & RENEWED

Healing Burnout and Finding Lasting Balance

SAMM SMELTZER
DMQ

Copyright © 2018, 2024 Samm Smeltzer
All Rights Reserved

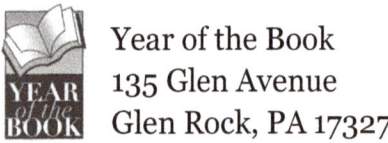
Year of the Book
135 Glen Avenue
Glen Rock, PA 17327

ISBN: 978-1-64649-446-0 (paperback)
ISBN: 978-1-64649-476-7 (ebook)

Library of Congress Control Number: 2025901726

Cover art by Jen Borror, www.hootdesignstudio.com

No part of this book may be reproduced or transmitted in any form or by any means, electronic or mechanical, including photocopying, recording or by any information storage and retrieval system without written permission from the author.

To those who unknowingly added weight to my healing journey:

Thank you. Your actions, though challenging, became the lessons I needed to rediscover myself, rebuild my energy, and establish the boundaries that now cultivate the peace I once thought impossible.

To the readers, may this book support you as you navigate your own lessons, affirming that you are never on this path alone.

Contents

PART ONE

1. Disengaged, Burnt Out, and Stuck 1
   - The Flamingo and The Phoenix 2
   - Employer–Employee Accountability 5
2. How to Read This Book 7
3. Composition and Progression of Burnout 11

THE ASSESSMENT

4. Directions 17
   - Assessment Results 35
5. The Five Levels of Burnout 37
   - Your Scores 37
   - The Progression of Burnout 38
   - Big Picture Observations 42
   - What's Next 43
6. Unpacking Work-Life Baggage 45
   - A Glimpse into Your Core: Visualization and Breathwork 47
7. Creating Your Core Map 51
   - Energetic Embryo Development 51
8. Beginning to Heal 57
   - Utilizing the Data Collected 58
   - Universal Truths to Return to 61
9. Lessons from the Stuck 63
   - You Caught My Eye 63
   - Doubting and Overthinking 64

10   Where to Start 69

     The Phase Calendar 71

PART TWO

The Wood Phase—Spring Season 75

     March..80

     April 84

The Earth Phase—Supporting Wood to Fire 91

     May 96

The Fire Phase—Summer Season 102

     June 107

     July 112

The Earth Phase—Supporting Fire to Metal... 121

     August.. 126

The Metal Phase—Fall Season 133

     September...137

     October 142

The Earth Phase—Metal to Water... 147

     November 152

The Water Phase—Winter Season 161

     December 166

     January.. 171

The Earth Phase—Supporting Water to Wood 181

     February 185

WHAT'S NEXT?

What's Next 195

Re-assessment 199

A Letter to You... 219

PART ONE

TAKE A
DEEP BREATH.

YOU ARE
EXACTLY WHERE
YOU NEED
TO BE.

1 | Introduction: Disengaged, Burnt Out and Stuck

When I left the traditional workforce a decade ago, I knew I was disengaged and stuck. What I didn't know was that I was burnt out. My business that was birthed at this same time, Leadership Arts Associates, was essentially a space holder for me to figure everything out. My husband had nudged me toward the entrepreneurial endeavor and genuinely wanted me to find happiness, but I felt so lost and numb and overwhelmed that this concept seemed elusive and impossible.

Recently an individual helped me find clarity about this time of my life. He suggested that if I could not articulate what was actually happening, then I would never truly be able to move forward. Amidst a busy evening reception filled with wine, appetizers, and small talk, this gentleman dove into a series of questions that he believed would illuminate the neurological pathway of clarity to solidify my healing and growth evolution.

The questions were intimate in nature, asking about my relationship at the time with my husband and my children. The conclusions included openly admitting that I had poured into my work while treating my family as secondary. He prodded at my definition of "success" and why I continually thought I never had it. In the end, there was one overwhelming call to action... for me to take ownership that *my employer did not burn me out. I did it to myself.*

The interaction left me bewildered. Looking back, I can't help but be proud of myself, not because of my responses, but because of how far I've come. I still stumble and definitely fall, yet getting back up is now easier and lighter. I no longer feel like there is a boulder on my back, which provided me justification to give up in the past. Things I once thought would haunt me for the rest of my life have been released and transformed into beautiful guideposts of growth.

When I was lost, numb, and overwhelmed, I was desperate for external intervention. I wanted someone to tell me what to do, and how to make it better. However, this survival tactic only caused me to become more lost, numb, and overwhelmed. I began to take every person's feedback as truth... telling me who and how I should be. And I tried to be all those things.

When I opened the doors to Leadership Arts Associates in 2014, it was a business filled with what everyone else wanted from me. I had no idea who I actually was, what I wanted, or even what I needed. If I had met this gentleman back then, the same interaction would have driven me to tears and that boulder would have grown ten pounds heavier.

If you're here because you're disengaged, burnt out, and stuck, you need to know that I am not going to be your external intervention. I wrote this book as a guide to help you heal yourself and find connected momentum again. It is important to recognize that this healing is not isolated to your work and professional identity; it will require all of you.

This book will be your roadmap, and it is filled with landmarks to help you know if you're heading in the right direction. Use this roadmap to tap into your own innate wisdom, and when you are finished, you will feel that inner guidance pouring out of you. You will be able to trust it with little or no doubt or resistance.

My hope is that this book gives you the space that Leadership Arts Associates gave me – the space to recognize where you are in this moment and to know that it can be different. And if your professional identity is your current whole identity and worth, like it was mine, then your starting point might simply be an invitation to pause. Set your intention to strictly cultivate awareness and recognition of your relationship with your inner and outer world.

That is when you will discover your balance, your flow, your way, your Dao.

The Flamingo and The Phoenix

The cover of this book displays the animal teacher for this work, a fusion of a flamingo and a phoenix. Let's take a moment and explore what guidance this bird can share for the work that is ahead.

The Vibrant Color of the Flamingo

Flamingos are known as those bright pink birds. Their color is a result of their food sources. They metabolize pigments that generate the color you see. For us, the lesson is as simple as: *You are what you eat.*

Connected directly to our work, that "food" equates to your priorities.

Red/pink is the color of the Fire phase and element. You'll be introduced to this concept in greater depth later. It is this element at the source and root of burnout.

Fire is tied to passion, things we are excessively excited about – like work, or the role as a parent, or even a hobby. The more you pour into this, the brighter and more vibrant the color.

Our culture praises this as "success." However, when this element becomes too vibrant, the Fire is too hot, and the flames burn you out like a phoenix meeting its death.

Noticing this vibrant color will allow you to reflect on your definitions of success, your priorities, and what pushes you too close to the flames.

The Fiery Death and Rebirth

The Phoenix is best known for its cycle of fiery deaths and rebirths. This is not much different than the cyclic evolution through healing and growth. Each fiery death should shed a layer that allows rebirth to a purer version of yourself.

However, these cycles also mimic what occurs when we get stuck. It feels as if we are reliving the same narrative over and over, only the character names and set change. The themes become repetitive. The fiery death is what happens when we simply can't do it anymore. Then we quit.

This cycle can only occur so many times until you find yourself exhausted and depleted, so much so that rebirth seems impossible.

The phoenix shows us the fine balance between what is and what could be. It's a shift that can be the difference between feeling trapped and flying free.

The Unseen Under the Wings

Underneath a flamingo's wings, you will find that they are black. You only get glimpses of this truth when the underpart of the wing is exposed. We all possess a darkness that we try to hide, or that we are afraid of. Avoiding this darkness could be what is perpetuating your current state of stagnation.

It is important to recognize that any aspect of yourself that you feel compelled to hide is still an essential piece of you. It holds the key to finding true balance in your life.

Balance is about recognizing and honoring your innermost self while also celebrating what has been cultivated. What you find lurking in that darkness is often you, in your truest, rawest form.

If that darkness feels scary, for known or unknown reasons, please seek additional support and guidance from a Mental Health professional to navigate that process. Choosing to ignore it, and moving forward with the work in this book, will deliver disingenuous results. Stagnant energy stops movement, and until the blockages are dissolved, it will continually cause obstructions.

Together vs. Alone

Flamingos are a community-based animal, whereas the Phoenix is typically a solo bird. I'd like to think that a hybrid of the two would create a bird that is strong on its own as well as in community.

The cycles of the Phoenix hint at a lonely and isolated path. Healing and growth can be accomplished on your own but are so much more powerful and sustainable when done together. You don't need accountability partners for a short-term challenge, but access to like-minded individuals will help you on an ongoing basis. This access is about seeking guidance, and more important, it's about cultivating strength and seeing that you are truly part of a greater collective.

We each have our own individual lives and unique circumstances, but there is a universal pulsating energy that connects us. Even though our challenges are not the same, there is a common thread that allows for understanding and support.

This is why I created the HRart Institute, a community focused solely on healing and growth. It is filled with like-minded individuals who resonate with this work at all different stages. I strongly encourage you to check it out via the link below. Simply be curious and engage only in the way you feel called. You'll feel the support merely by being in the space, but it also happens to be where you'll find the bulk of the resources referenced later in this book.

Go to **www.HRartInstitute.com**

Employer-Employee Accountability

Before we dive in, I feel it is important to address one more thing. In my introduction I mentioned my interactions with the gentleman who drilled into me that my burnout was my own doing.

The core of my work is with organizations. My mission is to reimagine the workplace so that it can become a nurturing environment for healing and growth. I believe this is a win for both employee and employer, allowing us to see possibilities on both sides.

That said, there is a level of accountability that only the employee possesses. As an individual who has the power of free will, you get to decide if you will be open to this possibility. Perhaps, you're not, and that's why you picked up this book… because you gave up all hope on the working world. If so, I wrote this book for you. There are those who feel like the corporate world has let them down in massive ways, that it is so cold and heartless that they abandoned their dreams.

When it comes to systems and the way we manage people, I do believe the working world is broken. I also believe the world is waking up to this fact. We must do things differently.

It is this combination of events that has created the opportunity for me to have a death and rebirthing cycle in my business – the death of Leadership Arts Associates and the rebirthing of The HRart Center. This is where we are doing the work, but if we are going to make massive shifts in this space, I need you to show up as well.

REST IS PART OF THE PROCESS.

ALLOW YOURSELF TO TAKE IT.

2 | How to Read This Book

This book is divided into two main parts.

The first is about your current state, recognizing with as much clarity as possible where you are today. You'll be guided through a series of exercises and assessments. Please move through this section intentionally with grace. Depending on your current state, these assessments may be disheartening and the exercises might feel challenging. Simply go through the motions, if you must, to get an initial baseline read.

The second part of the book is your roadmap for healing and growth. It will provide guidance for an entire year, teaching you how to use the data from Part One to target your healing for maximum impact.

At the end the book, we'll revisit a few of the earlier exercises and assessments to see how far you've come.

Before we dive in, there are few things to note in preparation as you move forward.

Grab a Journal

To get the most of this experience, you should use a journal, notebook or even a Word doc to log your experiences throughout the year. There will be immense value in your ability to look back later.

There is a journaling technique that was taught to me in grad school, that I found is an amazing method for capturing moments for future review. I call it the TFWN Method. TFWN stands for Thoughts, Feelings, Wants or Needs. When you encounter a moment that you want to capture, you will simply journal by free-writing for a minimum of 2-minutes and no longer than 5-minutes about one or all of the following prompts:

1. In this moment, what are you thinking?
2. In this moment, what are you feeling?
3. In this moment, what are you wanting?
4. In this moment, what are you needing?

There is no need to write or log the triggering event or moment that caused you to want to journal; answering the prompt for the suggested time frame is more than sufficient. Please try to avoid journaling longer than 5 minutes on any one prompt, as that typically transitions into venting and can be energetically depleting.

Note: If at any time throughout this journey you find the activity too difficult, challenging, or you are experiencing resistance... you can substitute a TFWN entry instead.

When You Feel Overwhelmed

I want to give you a simple exercise that you can return to at any time. It is likely that you will feel moments of overwhelm, from life, work, or even the idea of doing this work. This exercise is designed to ground you and regulate your nervous system. I want you to especially use it whenever you are feeling lightheaded or daydreamy. These are signs that energetically you are not present in your body and are likely just going through the motions of your day.

I've made a guided audio track of this exercise for your use at HRartInstitute.com. This is a great time to go and create an account there and get familiar with the portal, where you will have access to additional resources as well as a community of other readers on the same journey. When you sign into the HRart Institute, you'll want to find the Reader Support Center in the left-hand menu and then select *Unstuck and Renewed*.

Exercise: Rooted Through Breath

1. Sit comfortably in a chair with your feet flat on the ground.
2. Notice your breath, not attempting to control it. Notice the sensations of the breath entering your body and notice the sensations of the breath as it leaves the body.
3. Now bring your attention to your feet. Imagine your feet sinking into the floor, becoming one with the earth, providing a solid foundation.
4. From the bottom of each foot embedded into the earth, visualize the root reaching out and fully connecting you to the earth's core and its pure source of nourishing energy.

5. On your next inhale, imagine that tree root coming alive and beginning to absorb that earth energy, bringing it into your body through your legs. Allow your breath to bring this new grounding energy into your lower abdomen.
6. With each exhale, feel the new earth energy settle comfortably in the lower abdomen.
7. With each inhale, feel your lower abdomen becoming a bit fuller and heavier, allowing you to truly settle into your body.
8. Continue until your feeling of overwhelm has subsided, then you can gently lift your feet, disconnecting from the earth.

I Don't Feel Well Today

This book is a healing journey and therefore if you are sick or ill at any time while reading this book, please pause and care for yourself. Rest and heal physically, then return to this work. When you are sick, you should use all of your energetic reserves for that healing process.

Well, I think that's it. You're ready to get started.

Let's get you unstuck and renewed!

3 | Composition and Progression of Burnout

In 2019, the World Health Organization officially included burnout in the 11th Revision of the International Classification of Diseases (ICD-11). It was classified as a non-medical condition, an occupational phenomenon. According to this document:

> *Burnout is a syndrome conceptualized as resulting from chronic workplace stress that has not been successfully managed. It is characterized by three dimensions:*
>
> - *Feelings of energy depletion or exhaustion;*
> - *Increased mental distance from one's job, or feelings of negativism or cynicism related to one's job;*
> - *Reduced professional efficacy.*

The WHO went on to say, "burnout refers specifically to phenomena in the occupational context and should not be applied to describe experiences in other areas of life."

This definition should inspire a mixture of emotions. On one hand, it finally provides recognition to the very real impact that work can have on us, yet it encourages us to embrace a great divide of personal versus professional. The concept of "work-life balance" – *leaving work at work, and home at home* – is one of the primary drivers that accelerates the progression of burnout and exacerbates its symptoms. It is impossible to have feelings of depletion and exhaustion that are solely caused by work and not personal variables. Even if you were to create an extreme scenario of being isolated inside the work environment with no outside life, you are still a human being with personal needs; it is those needs that make this entire rationale unfeasible. You cannot and should not eliminate your humanity.

In the book *Five Element Constitutional Acupuncture*, authors Angela Hicks, John Hicks, and Peter Mole share that in Traditional Chinese Medicine, disease is viewed as the "breakdown of harmony within the body." The causes for this breakdown typically fall into three primary categories: internal, external, and miscellaneous factors.

- *Internal factors* are made up of what arises within us. They are how we process the world, our thoughts, and feelings.

- *External factors* are environmental and climatic conditions, like being too hot or too cold, shortened days in winter, and extra sunshine in summer.

- *Miscellaneous factors* include anything else, however they are predominantly comprised of your lifestyle. This includes everything from your current health, including diet and exercise, to your workload, and the toll that certain life experiences may have taken on you.

Burnout is a breakdown in the state of harmony within your body. From a Traditional Chinese Medicine (TCM) perspective, this is a form of dis-ease. Throughout my work, I have come to believe that the primary cause and progression of this disease is internal rather than external or miscellaneous. It is the way that we process the world, which is created and influenced by our life path.

However, the emotions and thought patterns that we navigate daily make us more vulnerable, so much so that your current level of burnout can be measured through your active emotional imbalances. These imbalances present themselves as physical, mental, and emotional symptoms that you are actively experiencing.

From an energetic perspective, physical symptoms are the manifestation of stagnated energy that has not been addressed. Typically the pathway begins as a thought form, then turns into an emotion attached to a thought pattern, which then turns into physical discomfort. The body is an amazing intuitive caretaker, using multiple avenues of communication to try to tell you that something is not right. Physical symptoms are its last resort – the body screaming for you to pay attention.

Before I introduce you to the five levels of burnout, let's pause and assess your current state and the imbalances that are feeding the active progression of burnout. You will be invited to retake this assessment later to see how your healing work has impacted your levels and phase imbalance composition. This will allow you to continue evolving your approach and restorative work.

A few things to note about this assessment:

- This activity includes a list of physical and psychological symptoms. We have been ingrained to associate burnout only with the professional environment, but please open your mind to release that separation, and instead see these symptoms as connected to your overall well-being. Keep in mind that you are the only one who will see your answers. Be honest with yourself, without any judgment, so you can cultivate the healing you most need right now.

- This assessment is quite extensive. My recommendation is to complete one section per day, to ensure you do not get assessment fatigue that will ultimately hinder your results. With that being said, the assessment is structured in a fashion that inquires first about the most pressing burnout symptoms.

- Each section has specific scoring directions to calculate totals and generate your results. However, <u>if you check less than three boxes in any one section</u>, the score for that section is automatically zero.

Let's begin.

IT'S OKAY
TO PAUSE

AND SIMPLY BE
IN THIS
MOMENT.

THE ASSESSMENT

4 | Assessment Directions

As you proceed through this assessment, you will encounter several lists of symptoms. It's important to note that these symptoms are indicators of possible energetic imbalances within your body and mind. An imbalance is neither inherently good nor bad; it simply signals areas where energy may not be flowing freely and optimally.

How to Complete the Assessment:

1. **Review each symptom listed carefully.**
2. **Check the box next to a symptom if:**
   - You are currently experiencing this symptom, OR
   - You have experienced this symptom at any time within the past year.

Special Note on Occasional Symptoms:

If you have experienced a symptom **only once** within the last year, consider the context:

- **Check the box if:** The symptom was significant enough to be memorable or if it impacted your day-to-day activities even briefly.
- **Do not check the box if:** The symptom was very minor, did not affect your daily activities, or seemed to be a one-off occurrence that you believe was tied to a specific and unusual circumstance (e.g., food poisoning, an accident).

Approach This Assessment with Openness

There are no right or wrong answers – only opportunities to better understand your needs. Each symptom checked helps paint a more detailed picture of your energetic health and can inform more personalized health and wellness strategies.

By carefully considering whether to check symptoms based on their impact and context, you contribute to a more accurate and meaningful assessment of your energetic balance.

Physical Water Phase Imbalances

For each symptom listed, check the box if the symptom is present now or if you've encountered it within the past year.

- ◯ Memory problems and trouble focusing
- ◯ Difficulties with movement and sensing changes
- ◯ Alterations in bone, joint, and dental health
- ◯ Issues with physical development and reproductive health
- ◯ Problems with managing body fluids
- ◯ Cysts, swelling, or hardening in reproductive and urinary organs
- ◯ Irregular sleep patterns, including trouble waking up
- ◯ Vision and hearing problems
- ◯ Ringing in the ears (tinnitus)
- ◯ Weakness and stiffness in the body and joints
- ◯ Wear and tear on spinal disks and cartilage
- ◯ Cold feelings in the lower body
- ◯ Need to urinate more often
- ◯ Bone thinning (osteoporosis)
- ◯ Early signs of aging (gray hair, hair loss, wrinkles)
- ◯ Fertility issues or sexual health problems
- ◯ Fatigue or low energy levels
- ◯ Reduced appetite
- ◯ Weakness in abdominal muscles
- ◯ Changes in skin color or texture
- ◯ Headaches, especially around the eyes or top of the head
- ◯ Decreased sweating and less frequent urination
- ◯ Stiffening of blood vessels and cartilage
- ◯ Kidney or bladder stones
- ◯ Development of bony growths
- ◯ Digestive issues

- ○ Receding gums (gum health problems)
- ○ Sleeping less than usual
- ○ Constipation or trouble with bowel movements
- ○ High blood pressure (hypertension)

Scoring for Section:

1. **Count the Symptoms**: If the total number of symptoms is less than 3, record a score of zero. If the total is 3 or more, note the total as the "Water Physical Phase Imbalance Score."
2. **Determine Burnout Level**: Take the "Water Physical Phase Imbalance Score" and multiply it by three. Add the result to the corresponding open slot in the tally table to determine the overall burnout level.

Total Score:

Energetic Water Phase Imbalances

For each symptom listed, check the box if the symptom is present now or if you've encountered it within the past year.

- ○ Social interaction challenges: You may find it difficult to engage in social activities or feel uncomfortable during social interactions.
- ○ Communication difficulties: You might struggle to clearly express your thoughts and feelings to others.
- ○ Discomfort in social exposure: You could feel uneasy or anxious when you are the center of attention or in large groups.
- ○ Critical behavior: You often find yourself criticizing others or focusing on their faults
- ○ Negative worldview: You tend to see the world in a negative light and often expect the worst outcomes.
- ○ Health anxiety: You frequently worry about your health and may be preoccupied with fears of becoming ill.
- ○ Immobility episodes: There are times when you feel so overwhelmed that you become physically immobile or emotionally unresponsive.
- ○ Observational preference: You prefer to watch others rather than participate in activities directly.
- ○ Imaginative thought processes: Your thinking often involves fantasy or unrealistic scenarios.
- ○ Financial frugality: You are extremely cautious about spending money, often to the point of avoiding necessary expenses.
- ○ Distracted by thoughts: You frequently find your mind wandering, and you have trouble focusing on the task at hand.
- ○ Intense observation: You tend to observe people and situations very closely, often noticing details that others miss.
- ○ Aloofness: You generally keep your distance from others and might come off as detached or uninterested.
- ○ Behavioral analysis: You often analyze people's behavior, trying to understand their motives and actions.

- ○ Unconventional behavior: Your behavior or thinking often deviates from the norm, and you are not afraid to be different.
- ○ Suspicion and covetousness: You may be overly suspicious of others' motives or envious of their achievements and possessions.

Scoring for Section:

1. **Count the Symptoms**: If the total number of symptoms is less than 3, record a score of zero. If the total is 3 or more, note the total as the "Water Phase Energetic Imbalance Score."
2. **Determine Burnout Level**: Take the "Water Phase Energetic Imbalance Score" and multiply it by two. Add the result to the corresponding open slot in the tally table to determine the overall burnout level.

Total Score:

Physical Wood Phase Imbalances

For each symptom listed, check the box if the symptom is present now or if you've encountered it within the past year.

- ○ Hypertension (including labile blood pressure)
- ○ Oily skin/hair
- ○ Boils
- ○ Muscle cramps in limbs
- ○ Vertigo
- ○ Hearing issues (including ringing in ears)
- ○ Spasmodic constipation
- ○ Sciatic pain
- ○ Pain in ribs
- ○ Heartburn
- ○ Swallowing difficulties
- ○ Eye and ear pain
- ○ Shingles
- ○ Increased clumsiness and susceptibility to accidents
- ○ Nail conditions (including dry, brittle, and thick nails)
- ○ Breast pain
- ○ Tendon conditions (including injuries and tendonitis)
- ○ Hypoglycemia
- ○ Blurry vision
- ○ Sensitivity to light and sound
- ○ Urinary tract issues (including cystitis, urethritis)
- ○ Itchiness in eyes and genital/anal areas
- ○ Joint and muscle conditions (including lax joints and tense muscles)
- ○ Irritable bowel syndrome
- ○ Chronic neck and shoulder tension
- ○ Headaches (including occipital and lateral)

- ○ Migraines
- ○ Jaw joint dysfunction (TMJ syndrome)
- ○ Facial nerve pain
- ○ Peripheral neuropathy
- ○ Sexual dysfunction
- ○ Menstrual issues (including painful cycles and PMS)
- ○ Substance abuse

Scoring for Section:

1. **Count the Symptoms**: If the total number of symptoms is less than 3, record a score of zero. If the total is 3 or more, note the total as the "Wood Phase Physical Imbalance Score."

2. **Determine Burnout Level**: Take the "Wood Phase Physical Imbalance Score" and multiply it by two. Add the result to the corresponding open slot in the tally table to determine the overall burnout level.

Total Score:

Energetic Wood Phase Imbalances

For each symptom listed, check the box if the symptom is present now or if you've encountered it within the past year.

- ○ Intense and forceful behavior: You often exhibit behavior that is aggressive or overly assertive, which can be overwhelming to others.
- ○ Lack of restraint: You find it difficult to control your impulses or refrain from acting on your immediate desires.
- ○ Difficulty in fair interactions: You struggle to engage in interactions that require fairness and equity, often prioritizing your own needs or views.
- ○ Challenges in collaboration: Working with others is difficult for you, especially when it involves compromising or sharing responsibilities.
- ○ Discomfort with uncertainty: You feel uneasy or anxious in situations where outcomes are uncertain or unknown.
- ○ Hostile behavior: You may frequently behave in a hostile manner, which can include being verbally or physically confrontational.
- ○ Overbearing attitudes: Your demeanor can be excessively controlling or demanding, often trying to impose your will on others.
- ○ Unpredictable or poorly considered actions: You tend to act without thinking things through, leading to unpredictable or rash decisions.
- ○ Inconsistent decision-making: Your decision-making process often lacks consistency, changing based on mood or external pressures.
- ○ Oppositional behavior: You regularly exhibit resistance or opposition in situations where cooperation is expected.
- ○ Domineering interactions: In your interactions with others, you tend to dominate the conversation or situation, often at the expense of others' participation.
- ○ Easily irritated behavior: You are quick to become irritated or annoyed, often over seemingly minor issues.

Scoring for Section:

1. **Count the Symptoms**: If the total number of symptoms is less than 3, record a score of zero. If the total is 3 or more, note the total as the "Wood Phase Energetic Imbalance Score."

2. **Determine Burnout Level**: Take the "Wood Phase Energetic Imbalance Score" and add the result to the corresponding open slot in the tally table to determine the overall burnout level. Recognize that this is the only phase that does not have a multiplier, this was intentional in the design.

Total Score:

Physical Fire Phase Imbalances

For each symptom listed, check the box if the symptom is present now or if you've encountered it within the past year.

- ○ Sleep disturbances
- ○ Heart conditions
- ○ Irregular heart functions
- ○ Circulatory system disorders
- ○ Facial complexion changes
- ○ Heat regulation issues
- ○ Sexual response issues
- ○ Skin conditions
- ○ Pulmonary hypertension
- ○ Painful urination
- ○ Anemia
- ○ Speech and sensation disturbances
- ○ Chest pain

Scoring for Section:

1. **Count the Symptoms**: If the total number of symptoms is less than 3, record a score of zero. If the total is 3 or more, note the total as the "Fire Phase Physical Imbalance Score."
2. **Determine Burnout Level**: Take the "Fire Phase Physical Imbalance Score" and multiply it by two. Add the result to the corresponding open slot in the tally table to determine the overall burnout level.

Total Score:

Energetic Fire Phase Imbalances

For each symptom listed, check the box if the symptom is present now or if you've encountered it within the past year.

- ○ Boundary issues: You often have difficulty setting and maintaining personal boundaries, which might lead to feeling overwhelmed or taken advantage of by others.
- ○ Pacing and stimulation management: You find it challenging to manage and maintain a comfortable pace in activities, often feeling either overstimulated or understimulated.
- ○ Anxiety about the unknown: You experience significant anxiety when faced with uncertain situations or future outcomes that are not clear.
- ○ Sleep disturbances: You frequently have trouble either falling asleep or staying asleep, which impacts your overall health and well-being.
- ○ Expression difficulties: You struggle to clearly express your thoughts and feelings, which can lead to misunderstandings or a sense of isolation.
- ○ Heightened startle response: You are easily startled by unexpected sounds or movements, more so than others.
- ○ Cognitive imbalances: You experience difficulties in your thought processes, which can manifest as disorganized thinking or difficulty concentrating.
- ○ Hypersensitivity: You are extremely sensitive to physical sensations, emotions, or social interactions, often feeling overwhelmed by them.
- ○ Social flirtation and seduction: You tend to engage frequently in flirtatious or seductive behavior, which may affect your social interactions.
- ○ Elevated emotional responses: Your emotional reactions are often more intense than the situation warrants, which can be draining for you and those around you.

- ○ Overly positive outlook: You maintain an excessively optimistic view, even in situations where such optimism may not be warranted.
- ○ Intense emotional feelings toward others: You often feel deep and overwhelming emotions toward others, which can affect your personal relationships.
- ○ Difficulty with emotional or physical detachment: You find it hard to detach yourself from situations or relationships, even when they are harmful or unfulfilling.
- ○ Excessive talking: You tend to talk more than most people, often dominating conversations or speaking without thinking about the impact on others.
- ○ Naivety in trust: You often trust people too readily, which can lead to disappointment or exploitation.

Scoring for Section:

1. **Count the Symptoms**: If the total number of symptoms is less than 3, record a score of zero. If the total is 3 or more, note the total as the "Fire Phase Energetic Imbalance Score."
2. **Determine Burnout Level**: Take the "Fire Phase Energetic Imbalance Score" and add the result to the corresponding open slot in the tally table to determine the overall burnout level.

Total Score:

Physical Earth Phase Imbalances

For each symptom listed, check the box if the symptom is present now or if you've encountered it within the past year.

- ○ Muscular and lymphatic dysfunction
- ○ Venous disorders
- ○ Digestive and appetite issues
- ○ Weight management difficulties
- ○ Fluid and secretion management issues
- ○ Tissue swelling and gland issues
- ○ General discomfort and pain
- ○ Reproductive and abdominal dysfunctions
- ○ Blood and vascular health issues
- ○ Eye and oral health issues
- ○ Swelling of internal organs

Scoring for Section:

1. **Count the Symptoms**: If the total number of symptoms is less than 3, record a score of zero. If the total is 3 or more, note the total as the "Earth Phase Physical Imbalance Score."

2. **Determine Burnout Level**: Take the "Earth Phase Physical Imbalance Score" and multiply it by 2.5. Add the result to the corresponding open slot in the tally table to determine the overall burnout level.

Total Score:

Energetic Earth Phase Imbalances

For each symptom listed, check the box if the symptom is present now or if you've encountered it within the past year.

- ○ Challenges with change and orientation: You find it difficult to adapt to new situations or changes in your environment, often feeling disoriented when your routine is disrupted.
- ○ Excessive caregiving or controlling behavior: You may engage in overly protective or controlling behaviors, often putting the needs of others before your own to an unhealthy extent.
- ○ Indecision and uncertainty: You frequently struggle to make decisions, feeling uncertain even when faced with relatively simple choices.
- ○ Self-identity and autonomy issues: You have difficulties maintaining a strong sense of self and often rely on others for validation or direction.
- ○ Focus and thought organization difficulties: You find it challenging to maintain focus or organize your thoughts effectively, which can interfere with completing tasks.
- ○ Dependency and pleasing behavior: You tend to depend too much on others for emotional support or approval and often act primarily to please others at your own expense.
- ○ Unstable thought and decision-making processes: Your thoughts and decisions may frequently change, lacking consistency and often appear erratic or poorly planned.
- ○ Emotional dependence and exaggerated affection: You exhibit a strong emotional attachment to others, often showing affection to an excessive degree that might not be reciprocated or appropriate.
- ○ Inability to progress or stabilize: You often feel stuck, unable to move forward or find stability in various aspects of your life, from relationships to career.

- ○ Interference in personal affairs: You may intrude into the personal matters of others, offering unsolicited advice or assistance, and overstepping boundaries.
- ○ Low energy and depressive states: You frequently experience periods of low energy and feelings of sadness or hopelessness that affect your daily functioning.
- ○ Invasion of personal space and boundaries: You might struggle with respecting the personal space and boundaries of others, often invading their physical or emotional space unintentionally.
- ○ Excessive worrying and conformity: You tend to worry excessively about various aspects of life and may conform to others' expectations or societal norms without true alignment with your own desires or beliefs.

Scoring for Section:

1. **Count the Symptoms**: If the total number of symptoms is less than 3, record a score of zero. If the total is 3 or more, note the total as the "Earth Phase Energetic Imbalance Score."
2. **Determine Burnout Level**: Take the "Earth Phase Energetic Imbalance Score" and multiply it by 1.5. Add the result to the corresponding open slot in the tally table to determine the overall burnout level.

Total Score:

Physical Metal Phase Imbalances

For each symptom listed, check the box if the symptom is present now or if you've encountered it within the past year.

- ○ Respiratory issues
- ○ Skin and integumentary issues
- ○ Fluid balance and hydration issues
- ○ Elimination system dysfunctions
- ○ Circulatory system problems
- ○ Nasal and sinus conditions
- ○ Sweat-related symptoms
- ○ Musculoskeletal rigidity
- ○ Emotional trigger-related symptoms
- ○ Cardiorespiratory reflections

Scoring for Section:

1. **Count the Symptoms**: If the total number of symptoms is less than 3, record a score of zero. If the total is 3 or more, note the total as the "Metal Phase Physical Imbalance Score."

2. **Determine Burnout Level**: Take the "Metal Phase Physical Imbalance Score" and multiply it by two. Add the result to the corresponding open slot in the tally table to determine the overall burnout level.

Total Score:

Energetic Metal Phase Imbalances

Place a check next to any symptom you are currently experiencing, or have experienced in the last year.

- ○ Control and authority issues: You often struggle with situations where you need to assert control or respond to authority, which may result in conflict or discomfort.
- ○ Difficulty with emotional challenges: You find it hard to manage and respond effectively to emotional stress, often feeling overwhelmed or unable to cope.
- ○ Relationship and intimacy difficulties: You experience challenges in forming or maintaining close relationships, often due to fear of intimacy or inability to connect on a deeper level.
- ○ Rigidity in perspectives and behavior: You tend to have a fixed way of thinking and acting, finding it difficult to adapt or consider alternative viewpoints or approaches.
- ○ Need for order and perfection: You have a strong desire for everything to be in order and perfect, which can lead to frustration when things do not meet your high standards.
- ○ Formal and prescribed behaviors: You often adhere strictly to formal rules or socially prescribed behaviors, sometimes at the expense of spontaneity or personal expression.
- ○ Superficial concerns and behaviors: You may focus on surface-level issues or engage in behaviors that lack depth and genuine engagement.
- ○ Discrepancies in beliefs and actions: There is often a gap between what you believe and how you act, which can lead to internal conflict or perceptions of hypocrisy.
- ○ Emotional responsiveness issues: You may have difficulties in responding appropriately to emotional cues or situations, often appearing detached or overly emotional.

- ○ Behavioral standards and conduct: You hold yourself and others to very high standards of behavior, which can lead to judgment or dissatisfaction with people's conduct.
- ○ Elusiveness in convictions: You might show a tendency to be vague or non-committal in your beliefs and opinions, often avoiding taking a firm stance on issues.

Scoring for Section:

1. **Count the Symptoms**: If the total number of symptoms is less than 3, record a score of zero. If the total is 3 or more, note the total as the "Metal Phase Energetic Imbalance Score."
2. **Determine Burnout Level**: Take the "Metal Phase Energetic Imbalance Score" and add the result to the corresponding open slot in the tally table to determine the overall burnout level.

Total Score:

Assessment Results

Active Imbalance Report

You will use this data later in the book.

Phase	*Physical*	*Energetic*	**Total**
Water			
Wood			
Fire			
Earth			
Metal			

Current Burnout Level

Water Phase Physical Imbalance Score **x 3**	
Water Phase Energetic Imbalance Score **x 2**	
Wood Phase Physical Imbalance Score **x 2**	
Wood Phase Energetic Imbalance Score **x 1**	
Fire Phase Physical Imbalance Score **x 2**	
Fire Phase Energetic Imbalance Score **x 1**	
Earth Phase Physical Imbalance Score **x 2.5**	
Earth Phase Energetic Imbalance Score **x 1.5**	
Metal Phase Physical Imbalance Score **x 2**	
Metal Phase Energetic Imbalance Score **x 1**	
Total	

GIVE YOURSELF
THE GRACE
TO REST.

5 | The Five Levels of Burnout

Now before we start to talk about what your scorecard means, it's important to make clear that this is and will be a journey. The scores generated by that assessment are not the result of one toxic workplace. They are a culmination of life events that likely started when you were a child.

As we talk about what's next, you'll soon realize how everything is connected and therefore requires time to heal. Personally, I've been healing for nearly a decade. Just last week my therapist told me she was worried about my well-being. Her exact words were: "It sounds like you're heading toward burnout." Honestly, I was mortified. I'm the healer of burnout. How could I be on the verge of burnout? I had to take a deep breath and remember that this is a journey, even for someone who has been immersed in the work.

Breaking habits that are so ingrained in how we live… to go-go-go a million miles a minute… leaves us little room to do the hard work. We must release thought patterns that trap us, and prioritize the work to rebuild personal energetic reserves, without being tempted to drain them immediately.

The reality is, most of us don't have the willpower to initiate change and fight against the grain. Not until we are burned out. The likelihood that you picked up this book because you're feeling good and simply want to feel even better is low. It's okay to be struggling, but you don't want it to overshadow your life or define it. You picked this book up because you hope there is another way.

And there is.

Your Scores

The scores from the assessment will serve you in two ways. First, they provide a checkpoint of where you are in this moment and give an idea of milestones for when you are heading in the right direction.

Typically, we rely on the concept of "feeling better" as affirmation of progress. Instead, this assessment gives you a list of physical and emotional symptoms associated with your current state. As you begin to no longer experience these symptoms, you can acknowledge tangible success.

The second way these scores serve you is by providing a roadmap for healing. Your scores will empower you to decide how you want this healing journey to unfold next.

The Progression of Burnout

From my work and research, I've been able to observe five stages of progression on the pathway to burnout:

Stage One:	**≤63**	Engaged
Stage Two:	**64-127**	Stressed
Stage Three:	**128-190**	Disconnected
Stage Four:	**191-254**	Disengaged
Stage Five:	**≥255**	Burned Out

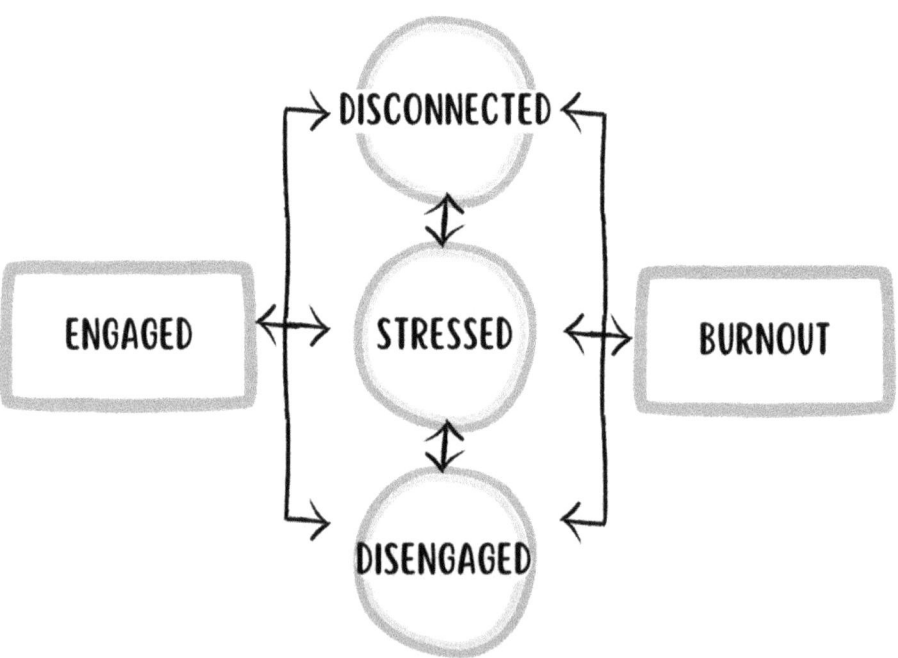

The Engaged Stage

This is the initial baseline for the pathology. At this stage, actively experienced imbalances are rather low. However, since this is the start of the burnout pathology, some signals of a possible progression are present. Symptoms can be seen in the relationship between the energy of the Heart and Kidney. This creates a dance between the emotions of excess joy and fear of the future.

From my work I have been able to draw a connection between the terminology of "professional passion" and excess joy. This passion is expected of engaged (from a traditional use of the word) individuals. There is even further expectation to fan this fire, which ultimately triggers excess joy. In this state, the energy begins to become loose and almost chaotic, which individuals often describe as stress associated with work.

This stress is not yet overwhelming, however, and therefore is not triggering an overwhelming depletion of energy. It is the chronic nature of this stress that plays a significant role in the progression to a further stage.

During this state, the individual experiences mild fear of the unknown future that interacts with the Heart energy, which masks it as excitement.

As long as the individual has entered the workplace without an imbalance in the area of sympathy and is receiving the necessary support to nurture their growth and confidence, the excitement can stay at a mild level without causing depletion of energy.

In contrast, if the individual actively has an imbalance in the area of sympathy, or the workplace causes an imbalance in that area, the masked mild fear will grow.

The imbalance of the emotion of sympathy is explained beautifully in the book *Five Element Constitutional Acupuncture*:

> Everyone needs support at times in their lives. People who did not feel sufficiently supported in their childhood tend to crave and demand an exceptional and inappropriate amount of support and caring later on in life. Alternatively they may find it very difficult to accept care and support from others. When they receive sympathy or support, it produces feelings of disquiet, rather than the feelings of comfort intended.

In extreme circumstances, the fear can be paralyzing in scenarios where the individual is not supported for an extended period of time. This development would lead to a further progression to the next stage.

The Burned-Out Stage

This stage represents the opposite side of the spectrum from the Engaged profile. Here it is expected that the individual will likely actively experience imbalances in all major emotional areas. The large scale of these imbalances is inevitably taxing the system, generating a level of exhaustion that makes the person feel barely functional.

The individual becomes angry and frustrated by an inability to materialize a desired change in the workplace. This emotional imbalance increases the level of cynicism as well as lowers the level of productiveness. Lack of joy and sympathy typically become imbalanced by a mutual lack of support and connection from the organizational culture, or a workload that prevents the individual from fulfilling these needs outside of the work environment.

The fear imbalance is fed by the potential future that awaits if the individual chooses to stay in the current environment. This ranges from fear of suffering and unhappiness to further loss of self or significant relationships that will be impacted by high levels of cynicism that carries outside work life.

Grief is the emotional imbalance that signals the severity of an individual's ability to re-engage. Often, this grief is centered around disappointment for what the organization promised it would be as part of the mutually agreed employment contract. This includes terms of employment but also the perceived work environment and culture that was promised.

The Stressed, Disconnected, and Disengaged Stage

To unpack these three stages from an energetic imbalance perspective, we must first examine the relationship between exhaustion, productiveness, and cynicism. Exhaustion is a measurement of the amount of energy present, while productiveness speaks to the level of free capacity remaining to function in life, including work. Cynicism levels speak to the individual creating energetic clusters through thought activity.

Dr. Jerry Alan Johnson, in his book *The Secret Teachings of Chinese Energetic Medicine,* describes this process of creating energetic thought forms. "Prolonged and persistent internal thoughts create and form energetic patterns. Then internal thought patterns become continually impregnated with the energetic charge of unexpressed toxic emotions, the energetic clusters will thicken, grow, and begin to create stagnation."

These in-between stages have varying degrees of the three components that map out the specific pathway of burnout progression for an individual.

Someone at the Stressed stage experiences low to moderate levels of exhaustion and cynicism, paired with low levels of productiveness. It could be possible that this individual began employment with a small amount of free capacity available. This limited capacity is now being drained as a result of negative energetic clusters that continue to grow, coinciding with increased levels of cynicism. This is where a "toxic work environment" is like pouring gasoline on top of a fire. The environment only encourages toxic emotions that thicken and grow energetic clusters, increasing stagnation.

Since low levels of productiveness are what is emphasized in this profile, the emotional imbalances that can be expected are around a lack of joy and sympathy. If confirmed, these emotional imbalances point toward workplace cultural issues surrounding lack of support and connection.

An individual at the Disconnected Stage experiences low to moderate levels of cynicism and productiveness, paired with high levels of exhaustion. If this person entered the workforce with an imbalance of excess joy, they would have a tendency to take on an excessive workload. This is possible to manage for a short period of time, but when it becomes the norm, it becomes a consistent drain on the individual's energetic reserves. Organizations that are understaffed, but unable to adjust to the demand, force individuals into circumstances of excessive workloads for an indefinite amount of time. As one continually loses energy to do the work, it is inevitable that levels of cynicism and unproductiveness will increase.

In this stage, I would expect to see a primary emotional imbalance of fear. However, in this scenario, the fear emotional imbalance is being triggered by the extreme low levels of energetic reserves. Therefore, the fear emotional symptoms will not necessarily be isolated to fear of the future but rather a general fear throughout all thought processes. This signals that the reptilian brain is beginning to guide the individual from a place of survival, with the primary goal of protecting limited energetic reserves. As a result, a tainted perspective is often adopted, viewing all possible life or work experiences as potential risks for suffering, encouraging the individual to avoid it as the best option for moving forward.

Another consideration at this stage is the individual's current energy level upon entering the employment environment. If the individual's energy level has already been significantly drained from prior employment with excess workload to an emotional taxing life experience, the person is beginning employment with only a limited amount of energy.

Finally, someone in the Disengaged stage experiences high levels of cynicism, paired with low to moderate levels of exhaustion and productiveness. This individual likely entered the workforce with established energetic clusters that are now being thickened by an external circumstance. It could be a toxic work environment, but more often is caused by particular scenarios that resonate with past toxic work environments experienced.

This stage speaks to a potential new hire employee who comes with past work-life baggage. If something is not done to help the individual process this baggage, it remains a stagnation that will only grow with small similar triggering events. In addition, the amount and act of suppressing these emotions will generate a consistent drain on the individual's energetic reserves, leaving them with less and less capacity to engage.

In this stage, I would expect to see emotional imbalances of anger, and a lack of joy and sympathy. This individual likely believes that change is impossible and struggles to develop meaningful relationships.

Big Picture Observations

When it comes to these three in-between stages, I've chosen to blend the discussion about them because it has proven difficult to identify solid themes at each individual stage. I believe this is because uniqueness demands fluidity. Therefore, before we move on, I want you to check in, acknowledging the following:

1. The higher your score is, the more burnout symptoms you are experiencing.
2. It is likely that you find yourself moving between the three in-between stages in a zigzag fashion. You may have one bad day, and then you have BAD DAYS. In other words, you are Stressed or DISENGAGED.
3. Instead of focusing on the specific stage, make note of what resonated with you in each of the stage descriptions. It is these details that will empower your forward movement.

What's Next

We are going to begin with some foundational healing around work-life balance. However, if you discovered in this chapter that you scored above 255 and are indeed in the Burned-Out stage, please pause here. It is vital that you reach out for professional help to guide you through your initial stages of healing. I highly recommend you start with your Primary Care Physician and allow them to guide you to appropriate next interventions.

HEALING

DOESN'T

HAPPEN

IN A HURRY.

6 | Unpacking Work-Life Baggage

Let's talk about this concept of work-life balance. For my work, I have begun to transition to a place of only discussing the idea of *balance* because the addition of the term *work-life* invites the imagery of a scale. If we took this imagery as truth that would mean that work and life are given equal privilege and right to our overall time and energy.

The global pandemic of 2020 was like lighter fluid on our way of living, lighting up what was, exposing the truth at the root. One of these exposed truths was that work should not dominate our lives. Therefore I don't even believe that work should have a right to 50 percent of our time and energy.

When I first wrote this book in 2018, I built it on the platform that on average, an individual will work 90,000 hours in a lifetime. To me, 90,000 hours seemed like too much time to spend miserable. However, now if I compare that statistic to the average number of hours in an individual's lifetime – 629,040 – I realize that 90,000 only makes up about 13 percent. Work truly is a small piece of our greater whole of living. This is also why I now believe that we have to make those 90,000 hours count... because your 90,000 hours could change the world. But you can only change the world if you are able to experience it fully, and to be present, showing up at your best.

I also think it's important to take a moment here and talk about the definition of work. What I am referencing is your primary occupation, where you mainly dedicate your work time. This definition is not limited to careers from a traditional sense, but roles that you agree to commit energy to. This could include parenthood, marriage (and long-term relationships in general), caretaking, and volunteering. These roles require energy just like a traditional job and therefore are work. Those who dedicate their time to multiple roles of this nature are indeed working the equivalent of multiple jobs. This is what comprises your 90,000 hours and if I had to take a guess, the long-outdated divide between work and life does not take into account this expanded definition. Therefore, I suspect your individual number of work hours may be a lot higher.

At the beginning of the previous chapter, I prefaced by saying this would be a healing journey. We are undoing layers like an onion, which have been forming since you literally left the womb. It is this undoing that is necessary for you to genuinely show up at you best.

In the conversations surrounding work life, the truth is that life is the foundation. Life – defined as your individual experiences in the external world and how you hold those experiences internally – is the basis for this work. Even though the layers started to form at birth, it is important to know that not everyone builds upon the same core. Each individual's core is unique and comprised of several things. Depending on your belief system, this could include generational trauma, past lives, karmic unresolved matters, and even hereditary disease... things that are passed on from generation to generation, or possibly lifetime to lifetime.

For me, I came into this life with anxiety and anger. Only recently did I learn of a family history of these, thus it now makes more sense, recognizing that my core already contained a seedling of anxiety and anger. These seeds were then fed by childhood social anxiety and friendship conflict. Minor acts of friend betrayal swirled in me with a rage that fueled grudges lasting from 4th to 8th grade. Anxiety about picture day led me to have meltdowns in the morning and panic attacks throughout the school day. It was easy to simply label me as a "sensitive child," which I was for other reasons, but these emotional upheavals were early signals of unprocessed stagnated energy building within.

I want you to start thinking about emotions as signals from your body, just like any other physical discomfort. When your body is in pain, emotionally or physically, it is attempting to communicate that something is not right. If we were to translate these signals into energetic definitions, physical discomfort would be a dense heavy stagnant energy, where emotional pain is a lighter almost cloud-like stagnation. One can become the other based on its level of stagnation. As an emotional energy becomes heavier, it can progress into a physical stagnation and vice versa. Therefore, these signals give you an idea of the healing progress occurring. Emotions will be part of this healing journey. It's inevitable. But as you begin to experience more emotion, you will also begin to experience more physical peace and lightness.

In this chapter, I want to give you a foundation for your core. I want you to see glimpses of where you truly started and what potentially is at the root of the layers.

In Classical Oriental Medicine, it is when we can identify and address the root that we have the ability to bypass healing each layer individually. We can instead heal the root and release those layers because they'll no longer have a point of attachment. To get a glimpse of this core, we are going to engage in a visualization and breathwork exercise.

This exercise will guide you to release stagnations that you are ready to let go of. Think of it like dusting off the cobwebs. You will then be invited to breathe in the virtues that should fill five powerful energy centers. During this exercise it important to not get caught up in what you should be experiencing. I give you permission to accept whatever happens for you as what should be happening for you. So even if you don't see anything, or feel anything, trust that the exercise is working within. While it creates its magic, make sure that you remain open and curious about whatever presents. This could be physical sensations or discomfort, random thoughts, or memories. Take them all in as 100 percent intentional. The more you embrace what presents, the more effective the outcome. This exercise will serve as a primer for our map.

Finally, make sure you have a journal nearby. At the end of this exercise you will be invited to free-write to capture your outcomes for later reference.

A Glimpse into Your Core: Visualization and Breathwork

An audio recording of this visualization is available to you in the Reader Support Center on the HRart Institute.

1. Find a quiet place and either sit or lay down, whatever will be most comfortable for you. If you lay down, make sure that you are not so comfortable as to fall asleep. If sitting in a chair, ensure that your feet are flat on the floor to ground you during the exercise.

2. Once you are settled in, begin tuning into your natural breath. Guide the breath in through your nose and out through the mouth. Allow the natural rhythm and flow of your breath to continue. As the

breath enters the body, send it down to your belly, filling the belly. As you exhale out through your mouth, release the air from your belly. Continue breathing in this fashion, focusing on filling the belly fully on the inhale and emptying the belly fully on the exhale.

3. We are going to begin our visualization by focusing on the Wood Phase. Imagine that the breath of your inhale transforms into a beautiful emerald green mist. Breathe in this emerald green mist and feel it travel into the chest, passing through the heart, belly, and into the lower abdomen. As the mist passes through each area, feel the virtues of love, kindness, and compassion filling you within.

4. Now begin to exhale out of the mouth, seeing a turbid green being released. In this turbid mist, any feelings of anger, rage, irritation, and jealousy that no longer serve you are released. Continue breathing in the emerald green, filling with the virtues of love, kindness, and compassion, and exhaling the turbid green mist. With each exhale you notice that the turbid green mist becomes a bit lighter and brighter. Continue until the turbid green mist has transformed into the emerald green mist.

5. We will now focus on the Fire Phase. The emerald green mist transforms into a beautiful ruby red. You invite this ruby red mist into your body and feel it fill within. As it passes through the heart, belly, and lower abdomen, you feel it filling you with the virtues of joy, contentment, peace, and tranquility.

6. Begin exhaling out the mouth a turbid red mist. Release with it any feelings of nervousness and excitement that no longer serve you. Continue filling and releasing until the turbid red mist transforms into a ruby red.

7. Start transitioning to the Earth Phase. The ruby red mist transforms into a golden yellow mist. Begin filling the heart, belly, and lower abdomen with this golden yellow. As you invite this mist into your body, you feel it filling with the virtues of trust, openness, and acceptance.

8. Exhale out a turbid yellow mist, releasing with it any feelings of worry, remorse, regret, obsessiveness, and self-doubt that no longer

serve you. Continue filling and releasing until the turbid yellow mist transforms into the golden yellow.

9. Moving on to the Metal Phase, the golden yellow mist transforms into a bright white mist. Breathe it in and fill the heart, belly, and lower abdomen. As you invite this bright white mist into the body, you feel the virtues of righteousness, dignity, and integrity.

10. As you exhale the turbid white mist, release any feelings of grief, sorrow, anxiety, and despair that no longer serve you. Continue until your exhaled mist has transformed into a beautiful bright white light.

11. Finally, let's move to the Water Phase. The bright white mist transforms into a deep navy-purple. Breathe in this deep navy-purple mist, filling your heart, belly, and lower abdomen. As you fill within, you feel the virtues of self-confidence, inner strength, and power.

12. Begin exhaling out a turbid, almost black mist, releasing any feelings of fear, insecurity, and loneliness that no longer serve you. Continue filling and releasing until the turbid black mist becomes the vibrant deep navy-purple of the inhale.

13. We will now move into the free-write portion of this exercise. Grab your journal and writing utensil. Answer the following prompts with whatever free-flowing thoughts come to mind. Let go of what the answer should be and trust that the answer which comes is what it needs to be.

    - When was a time that you desired love, kindness, and compassion, but instead experienced anger, rage, irritation, or jealousy?

    - When was a time that you desired joy, contentment, peace, and tranquility, but instead experienced nervousness and excitement?

    - When was a time that you desired trust, openness, and acceptance, but instead experienced worry, remorse, regret, obsessiveness, and self-doubt?

- When was a time that you desired righteousness, dignity, and integrity, but instead experienced grief, sorrow, anxiety, and despair?
- When was a time that you desired self-confidence, inner strength, and power, but instead experienced fear, insecurity, and loneliness?

It's now time to take a pause. Let the experience of this visualization exercise integrate for at least 48 hours before moving on. While integrating, you can begin preparing for the next step which will require magazines. In the past I've given alternative methods to completing that exercise, however none have quite the same impact. Therefore, go visit your grocery store and pick out 3 magazines or more. Don't be afraid to choose magazines that appear to be calling to you. Keep in mind that these will be tools in your healing journey, not personal reading material.

7 | Creating Your Core Map

Instead of beginning this section by thinking about your core self, I invite you to instead think about your pure self. Pure, being a word that hopefully inspires images of a version of you before it was ever tainted or influenced by external factors. Pure, being a state similar to infancy. Pure, being the clear purpose for your existence in this present moment.

Energetic Embryo Development

It was in my very first Medical Qigong training class that I learned about this topic. Energetic Embryo Development is the study of how your energetic self comes into being at conception and birth. It is this energetic body that allows you to come to life beyond simply a heartbeat and breath. It allows you to feel, think, and dream. Your energetic body develops according to a blueprint that is comprised of several elements, but two of which happen to be the focus for our work in this chapter.

These two elements are what I will be calling the Original Heart and Acquired Heart. As you may suspect they are both attributes of the Heart, which is where I would visually like you to imagine your physical "core." However, when adding the idea of the Heart to this visualization, I'd like you to embody the concept of Heart on all levels that resonate with you. Yes, think about the physical beating organ, but also invite your thoughts of it including your soul or higher self.

The relationship between this Original Heart and Acquired Heart speaks directly to the personal growth and healing that we are tackling in this present moment. It speaks to the tension between your Original Heart that is desperate to share your pure purpose for being and the Acquired Heart's logical arguments for why this purpose sounds impossible or unreasonable. It's the beautiful dance of free will and dreaming. It is in this dance that we begin to first experience imbalances – imbalances that then become greater, as they fuel the Acquired Heart's analytical processing.

These are the same imbalances that build and become the manifestation of burnout at the five levels. It is almost as if the great source of imbalance comes right here at the core, between the Original and Acquired Heart. It's less a lack of balance between work and life and more a lack of balance between who we are and what we think we should be.

The healing journey will be about exploring your untamed Acquired Heart and re-establishing a healthy relationship with this side of yourself. However, before you can do this, you must remember who you are at the core; you must see your Original Heart… or at least see as much as you humanly can at this moment. I know this might sound like an impossible task, especially because you picked up this book at a time when you probably feel the least like yourself.

The idea of even trying to answer any question regarding true identity or purpose seems overwhelming. Well, take a deep breath because I'm not going to ask you to do any of that. In fact, the only way we can materialize the Core Map is by you letting go. Release all expectations of what should happen, or what it should be. This creative process is going to tap at a depth within you that can be subconsciously guided. Therefore, the biggest obstacle will probably be that very loud overactive Acquired Heart that clearly knows everything and therefore will continually interrupt this process, judging you and criticizing you in the worst ways possible. You'll hear the whispers and ruminating thoughts of *what's the point, why bother, this is stupid.* Instead start to recognize these thoughts and words as cues that you're on the right path. In fact, the more frantic the Acquired Heart is, the closer you are to hearing the Original Heart. Think of your poor imbalanced Acquired Heart as an attention-demanding toddler who will throw a tantrum when being continually ignored. But this step is not about the Acquired Heart. It's about making space for the Original Heart to be heard.

Step 1. Collecting Images

Are you ready for your Acquired Heart to start piping up? Because let's cue that voice right about now. Your subconscious self has already been at work since you picked up this book. It perhaps was even the reason why you encountered it in the first place. So, as you have been reading along, your subconscious self has been working away and you are 100 percent ready for this next step. You simply need to trust yourself. I know... easier said than done.

For this step, you'll need those magazines that I prompted you to collect at the end of the previous chapter. This step might take you an hour or it could take you a week, and I cannot reiterate enough that you should take all the time you need. If you really can let go and trust yourself, you'll know when this step is actually complete. If you're struggling to let go, know that at least an hour will be a sufficient starting point.

During this time, I invite you to browse the magazines and pull out any images or words that appear to speak to you. Feel free to use that time to trim the images or words down, isolating strictly what spoke to you. That's it. This step is about collection, creating a pile of visual messages from the Heart. Don't get caught up pondering whether it's from the Original or Acquired, just recognize when the Heart speaks and collect.

Now if you find yourself at times struggling because the Acquired Heart's words are so deafening, please understand this as a signal to pause your collection practice. This does not necessarily signal that this practice is complete, but you may need to pause and return later. This is why I referenced that the practice could take a week.

Step 2. Sort Images by Color

Your next task is to sort your collection of magazine clippings by color. Your mission is to arrange them all into the five following color categories:

1. Red, Bright Orange, Pink
2. Yellow, Golden, Tan, Brown, Beige and Light Orange/Clay
3. Black, White, Metallic, Grey
4. Navy, Blue, Purple
5. Green, Teal, Turquoise

As you look at each of your magazine clippings, sort them into the corresponding category that represents the dominant color of the item. This could be the primary color in the image or font text, or it could be the color that stands out to you the most.

Step 3. Create Your Map

We are now going to begin building your map. To do this, you're going to need a canvas. My personal recommendation would be to make a trip to your local art store and invest in an actual canvas; the size is completely up to you, however I would not recommend anything smaller than 16" x 20" because have space to play will be helpful. However, if you want to use paper or some other creative medium as your canvas, go right ahead.

Once you have acquired your canvas, begin placing your image collection using the template below.

	Red, Bright Orange, Pink	
Green, Teal, Turquoise	Yellow, Golden, Tan, Brown, Beige and Light Orange/Clay	Black, White, Metallic, Grey
	Navy, Blue, Purple	

This template places the yellow collection of images in the center of your canvas, with the other four collections circling around, almost flowing one into another.

As you play with placement, pay attention to the following:

1. If you feel like at any time you are forcing an image from your collection to fit on the canvas, you have permission to set that image aside or completely let it go. Nothing should be forced into placement.

2. If you notice that you no longer feel anything for an image while you are placing it, then let it go. This happens for a multitude of reasons, but long story short, if an item doesn't feel like it belongs, it probably doesn't.

3. If you feel some of the images are more messages from your Acquired Heart rather than Original Heart, like they somehow sneaked in, then set them aside. Once identified, you should acknowledge that they don't belong on your Core Map.

Play with the placement of the images until it feels right, or you feel as though it's as good as it's going to get. Remember, this is about honoring where you're at in this moment without judgment. The Original Heart might be hard to hear, as its messaging might be coming in a bit foggy. This map is not about perfection; it is about presence. It's about being in this moment and owning what you can see and hear in this moment.

Once you've finished placement, attach your images using glue – or my personal favorite, rubber cement – and then set the canvas aside. We'll revisit it in the next chapter, but make sure you rest and allow the work you've just done to settle before moving on and turning the page.

This is Too Much: An Alternative Method

If creating this Core Map feel like an overwhelming task, which is likely if you are experiencing a later stage of burnout. I'd like to provide you with an alternative simpler version.

1. Pick up the magazines and flip through until you find five images that catch your eye.

2. Then flip through the magazine and find five words or phrases that resonate or speak to you.

3. See if it feels right to pair certain words and images together. Keep your sets and this collection of images and words for the next step.

TRUST
IN YOUR
PAUSES.

8 | Beginning to Heal

Over the last few chapters, you've collected a lot of data – information about where you are in this present moment. Not only does this collection process serve as a benchmark, but we are now going to use that data to determine the path forward.

One of the biggest challenges when it comes to healing burnout is that the method or protocol must meet the person where they are at and travel with them on the journey, able to adapt accordingly for bumps and obstacles that will be uniquely yours.

Therefore, what's next could not be provided in a start-here/end-here fashion. Instead, it will be presented in a manner you can navigate to find what you need, when you need it, placing you in complete control of this healing journey. This might sound overwhelming, but that's why we are going to take the time here to prepare you for what's ahead.

For this journey, you'll need essentially three things:

1. An understanding of the data you've collected
2. Some foundational rules for diving in
3. Your initial launching point

Before we begin, I want to invite you to take a moment and check in with how you are feeling at this point in the journey. Our work until now has only established a baseline; healing and growth are what's coming. That said, the collection of resources we used to establish the baseline of your current state was likely accompanied by some challenges. There is a reason I have continually prompted you to slow down and take your time. Each assessment and exercise evaluated your energy at different levels. The final activity, creating your Core Map, was an assessment of your spiritual energetic imbalances, meaning it required you to reflect at the deepest levels. If you are experiencing burnout, this level will be the most difficult to tap. That being said, this is your baseline and you'll be amazed even at the smallest shift in ease you gain when attempting to repeat this exercise after beginning your healing path.

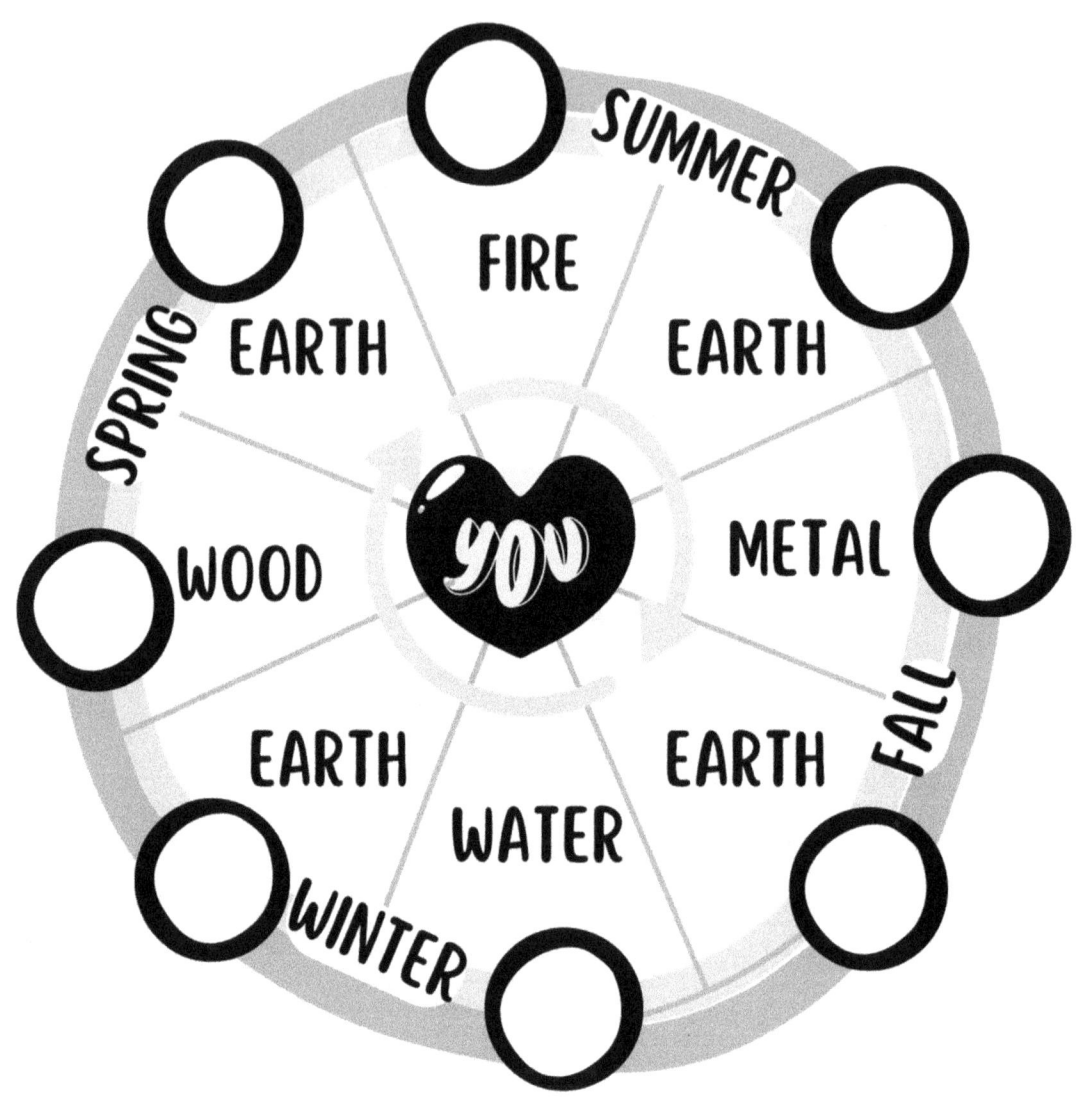

Utilizing the Data Collected

The data you've collected through the exercises in these chapters contain two major revelations. The first is where you should focus, and the second is where it will be the hardest.

To decipher these revelations, you will need to have your Burnout Assessment Results, your free-writing response from the visualization exercise, and your Core Map. Then follow the instructions below:

1. Examine your Burnout Assessment Results and identify which Phase has the highest total number of Active Imbalances. To determine this, it might be helpful to translate your Phase Imbalance Scores into the chart on the previous page. The Earth score should be repeated four times, to give you a clear picture of how these scores relate to one another. Then color the phase with your highest total number of imbalances. If you have a tie for the highest total number go ahead and color both phases.

2. Reread your free-writing responses after the visualization exercise. Identify which prompt generated the highest release – meaning that you had no trouble thinking of a time when the desired behavior you were seeking was not met. Then match that prompt to its corresponding phase in the chart below. Finally, color that phase on the graphic on the previous page.

Desired Behavior	Phase
love, kindness and compassion	Wood
joy, contentment, peace and tranquility	Fire
trust, openness and acceptance	Earth
righteousness, dignity and integrity	Metal
self-confidence, inner strength, and power	Water

3. Now, look at your Core Map and reflect on the following:
   - Did you intuitively collect images that fell in all five categories? If not, which color categories are not represented?
   - Are any color categories stronger than others? Is there one that seems to be overwhelming the map?
   - In contrast, is there a color category that only minimally fulfills the requirement? Or perhaps you feel like the image placement was a stretch.

- Overall, what areas of the map feel massively incomplete or bothersome?
- Lastly, is there any specific color that seems to be threaded throughout the map? For example, you might have an image of a dog that is black and white that you positioned on the right side of your map but now notice that it has hints of green in the background. After noticing these accent colors, you may begin to realize there are hints of green throughout the entire map, not strictly isolated to the left side.

Taking into consideration your responses to these reflective prompts, identify the top color category that is present on your canvas. Then use the chart below to identify which phase that color category corresponds with. Then color that phase on the graphic on the previous page.

Colors	Phase
Green, Teal, Turquoise	Wood
Red, Bright Orange, Pink	Fire
Yellow, Golden, Tan, Brown, Beige and Light Orange/Clay	Earth
Black, White, Metallic, Grey	Metal
Navy, Blue, Purple	Water

4. Take a moment to focus on the relationship between these three results.
    - Are all three from the same phase?
    - If they aren't, how did the other phases show up in alternate exercises?

The phases you've identified in the chart above are the phases that you should plan to focus on during this next portion of our work. Note, however, that these will also be the phases where you'll experience the greatest struggle.

In addition, let's now add in your Burnout Assessment Level Score. The higher your score, the harder this next step will potentially be.

The challenges and struggles that await are not a result of the tasks themselves being hard, in fact you'll find most are rather simple. The struggle comes from the combination of limited capacity and very active energetic imbalances.

The higher your Burnout Level, the more limited your capacity, which means you just won't have the energy to expend on healing right now. Therefore, as you dedicate what little reserve you have left to this process, your body will resist because it wants you to rest. Sometimes your baseline healing will be sleep.

On top of that, your active energetic imbalances can cause a bit of chaos. Sometimes your body, from a well-intentioned place of protection, will make you have the feelings or thoughts that generate self-sabotage. The answer to this occurrence is not to force your way through; it's likely that you won't be able to. It's more important to have the awareness that this saboteur talk can and will happen, and the mere recognition of it will provide perspective, allowing you perhaps to see the feelings and thoughts as imbalances rather than truth. This will become easier as you continue this journey, knowing that each step forward pulls back yet another layer. With each step you literally are getting lighter and clearer. This brings me to our next piece of preparation – foundational rules.

Universal Truths to Return to

Here are a few rules to keep in mind as we venture into this healing journey. These rules are a sort of universal truth, so as you move forward, know that you can rely on them as your foundational guidance. Feel free to return to them any time you find yourself being challenged beyond your current capacity; these guideposts will provide a path for continued momentum.

1. When it comes to lack of capacity, the number one recovery resource is sleep. If you are struggling with the capacity to begin an activity, let it go for the time being and rest. This includes going to bed early and even finding a way to take afternoon naps. If you are struggling to find time in your day to focus on a task, do not sacrifice your sleep.

Your sleep comes first and then other activities. Trust that when you are well rested, your sleep schedule will adjust, and time will be gifted once again. Don't worry... you will not be sleeping forever, even though at the beginning it might feel like that.

2. Emotional releases and healing can happen in waves. There is no requirement or prize for aggressively trying to move through all your emotional muck in one exercise or sitting. Be gentle with yourself and provide permission for pauses. That said, when an emotional release surfaces, it is highly recommended that you move the energy through rather than stopping amidst and possibly causing an uncomfortable stagnation. This means to keep going and complete the exercise rather than abruptly stopping in the middle.

3. Change will only come with consistency over time. This will never be a 30-day extreme energetic makeover. To truly heal, it will take time. With that being said, we are playing a long-term game. If you deviate from "ideal plans" for one day, it is not a complete derailment. Instead, view those days of deviation as honoring yourself and where you are at in that moment, knowing that tomorrow or even the following week you can choose again to be intentional with this journey.

4. In the world of cultivation, more advanced activities do not necessarily mean greater outcome. You'll be exposed to a variety of methods for navigating your healing. Know that sometimes simpler is better. Those other methods will be there when you're ready. Regardless, the activity or exercise should never feel daunting or exceptionally uncomfortable. I'm a fan of playing with edges, but not tossing yourself into the deep end.

5. Nothing should ever feel forced, and you should never fight what feels natural. Please do not concern yourself with thoughts like *am I doing this right?* Trust yourself to know what is right for you. View the activities like prompts of inspiration to get you heading in the right direction. You should never feel guilt, shame, or doubt because of a modification or even substitution. This whole thing will only work if the path aligns with you at the deepest levels, and only you truly know what that will take.

9 | Lessons from the Stuck

I spent a lot of time thinking about what I could offer you at this stage of the book, knowing that you'd probably only be reading from within a few different scenarios:

1. You are flipping through the book and the title of this section caught your eye.
2. You're overwhelmed by the amount of work and are basically procrastinating or trying to determine if you even want to start.
3. You've been doing the work, but you feel exactly the same.
4. You've finished an entire year of growth and healing and are asking what's next.

I thought the best way to address each of these different scenarios was to unpack them through the lessons of individuals I've encountered who have been stuck at these different stages. We'll explore why each experienced their stagnation and how to possibly move forward.

You Caught My Eye

The whole reason I was so determined to do a new edition of *Unstuck U* was watching how many people were drawn to the title. It is by far the one book of mine that people walk by and make comments like, "Unstuck U? I'm stuck – sounds like something I need!" I then watch these individuals purchase the book without even glancing through it or inquiring what it is really about.

Being stuck is clearly a concept that resonates with many. However, deciding to actually pay attention and take steps toward becoming unstuck is quite a milestone. It demonstrates a level of awareness where you're ready to articulate it and own it, which then creates the primer for doing something about it.

I've run into a few of these individuals who have purchased my first edition over the years. When I ask them if it was helpful, most openly admit that the book went on a shelf and they've never looked at it. Occasionally, they consider looking at it and a few have even pulled it off a shelf or the nightstand for a period of time before returning it to the bookcase. As grateful as I am for every book purchase, I do write in hopes that this information will serve those who need it. Perhaps having a shelf reminder at this time might be of service to you. Or perhaps this caught your eye and it gave you the words to describe where you are right now for the first time. Suddenly you're open to exploring the possibility of finding a way to experience movement and momentum again.

The next few points I think will paint a pretty clear picture of whether this book is a possible path for you to explore further. And if the answer turns out to be no, I hope it also gives you the space and permission to put this book down and go find a resource that will resonate with you to continue with your small step forward.

Doubting and Overthinking

One of my favorite ways to share the knowledge from this book is by teaching the Medical Qigong Practitioner Training Program inspired by the lineage of Dr. Jerry Alan Johnson. The first two courses out of eight in this curriculum focus on providing a foundational understanding of most of the concepts touched on in this book.

Every time I teach the first two-day course, the reaction is the same. People are overwhelmed by the amount of information. The only exception is from those who have already been studying Chinese Medicine for some time, in any form. I think the organic reaction of overwhelm is due to the mere fact and acceptance that we are exploring a whole new world of energetic anatomy, philosophy, and theory. It truly is a specific course of study that can take a lifetime to learn. Even though this is a form of energy medicine, it cannot be treated as a quick add-on to other modalities. In order to embody and gain the benefit from this modality and ancient teachings, it must be approached with a high level of respect – not demanding that you agree with all of it, but at least open to hearing how this work has served so many for over 5,000 years.

Often, I find that the individuals who really struggle with respect and openness have an imbalance in two aspects: a deficiency of faith and an excess of fear.

A Deficiency of Faith

When this imbalance is present, I find that individuals encounter this work, Medical Qigong, or this book because of a recommendation. Someone who has experienced a positive outcome recommends that perhaps you try it as well. Sometimes that means you're even gifted this book. At the end of the day, you must have some sort of genuine faith or belief that this is good for you. Faith is not from a religious perspective, but simply a genuine belief. You don't have to understand it or even be energy sensitive, but you need to have an inner knowing of some sort that this is meant for you, and worthy of your time. This creates a baseline motivation to get started and it also will serve as your continued motivation as you take on this journey that requires commitment.

An Excess of Fear

This imbalance appears most commonly in two scenarios. The first is from being exhausted and extremely depleted energetically. Your energetic system will turn on survival mode and utilize fear to minimize your use of energetic reserves. Its intent is to keep you safe, by encouraging you to stay where it is comfortable, easily saying no to decisions that require the use of more energy. This could include social invitations, so as a result you begin to isolate. It could also reject invitations to heal or grow, making it easier to just not try. This is why at my practice I continue to provide Medical Qigong Table Sessions, when you can invite a practitioner to do the work found in this book for you. While laying clothed on a massage table, a Medical Qigong Practitioner is able to balance the energy.

The other scenario happens for those individuals who have been on a self-healing journey for a while. They've been playing, exploring, and working on their energy with different types of modalities and maybe even practitioners. The framework for Chinese Medicine has commonalities and connections to other energy modalities, but also provides insight into spaces that previously had no guidance. This often causes a level of defensiveness as the individual questions what this new information means in terms of their journey to this point. Energy is energy, and despite that Medical Qigong is my chosen modality of practice, I also spent many years working with other practitioners. This knowledge has only deepened my understanding of myself and the work that I do. I believe it can do the same for you, if you are able to let down the guard of sorting through who's right and what's wrong. Instead, see it as another ancient text ready for your translation to take and absorb what is meant for you, and leave all the rest. If you stay with your guard up, you'll have inevitable resistance, even at a subconscious level, and you'll pretty much self-sabotage the work, to essentially prove you're right.

There is another reason. I believe people are overwhelmed at first exposure to these concepts. These lessons are tied to the Dao, which is translated as "the Way." It offers a way of life that invites balance, one that is counterintuitive to how we have glamorized self-help as a society. We are obsessed with quick fixes that invite extreme shifts to produce results in short time frames. This instead very much plays a long-term game. It asks us to linger in a space of mediocrity. Not too much or too little of any one thing, with invitations to present and work through only an aspect of the greater whole at a time. This approach creates a shift toward a lifestyle that has the ability to nurture and balance you on an ongoing basis.

I also want to invite you to have grace with yourself. If you struggle with the consistency of the daily or weekly activity presented in the book, that's okay. Don't use that as a measurement of your success or failure. Consistency is about returning over and over again to the practices for the long haul. Even if it's a month or months since your last return, celebrate every time you choose to engage with the work. The consistency of daily and weekly will come, and you will find the innate rhythm that is yours for continued balance and evolution.

I Don't Feel Anything

Some of this can be the result of the previously mentioned glamorization of the self-help industry. Some of us have gotten really good at plowing through self-help tasks, to the point that we are almost just going through the motions. It has numbed us and our ability to dig deeper. We begin to ignore suggestions, thinking, *I've done all this already*. The one thing I will say is that the sequence and consistency of these practices are what make it effective. Nothing really began to shift for me until I embraced consistency. Even if you have a daily practice of meditation or yoga, I challenge you to check in and make sure your practice still resonates with you. You need to feel connected during that time in order for it to work and care for your energy.

The other reason people don't experience shifts or struggle to feel energy is because they hit a block, typically not at the surface. Therefore, you're likely to be thinking, *This isn't me, I'm not blocked*. This is the time when I do recommend that you seek out an additional resource – a therapist, psychologist, psychiatrist, or another form of trauma-related therapy. These blocks commonly are related to trauma and I've seen them on the entire spectrum, even tied to suppressed memories that individuals can't even recall. These blocks play a role in your overall stagnation. This becomes an area where energy is unable to move or flow freely. In addition, they become a magnet for similar vibrational energies, as like attracts like. I've seen this enough times over the years that I strongly urge you to not let this block become the reason you stop your journey. Reach out and find support. Find a place that feels safe with someone who can guide you through the fear to dig a bit deeper.

SLOW DOWN.

THE NEXT STEP
WILL WAIT FOR YOU.

10 | Where To Start

The last piece we have to cover is where to start and how to navigate this next part.

The greatest teacher for finding balance is nature, particularly the seasons. As the seasons change, nature is prompted to grow and evolve. This is done by subtle vibrational requests that even we feel at a deep level. If we can take a step back and allow nature to be the guide for our growth and healing journey, we'll find ourselves with an innately organic map for the year. Allow the seasons to dictate your path, timing, and focus areas… one that does not demand highly aggressive deadlines, and is void of built-up pressure to a drastic conclusion or climax. Instead, this journey gently requests your presence to explore certain aspects of yourself for a season each year.

In order to get you started experiencing this natural growth calendar, and in an effort to keep the initial path markers simple, we are going to use the current season to determine where you will start. The calendar at the end of this chapter will direct you to the appropriate phase based on the month when you are beginning.

Please note that the seasonal/month correspondence reflects those of the Northern Hemisphere and will therefore need to be adapted if you live in the Southern Hemisphere. I have listed the season in the calendar, to hopefully help you with any modifications that might be necessary.

Once you locate your starting Phase, you will find that chapter in Part Two. There you will be given specific directions for caring, nurturing, and healing that phase. These directives will be given in weekly timeframes. Here are a couple of helpful hints to help you get settled into the flow:

Here are a couple of helpful hints...

- If you are starting in the middle of a month, do not jump to week 2 or 3. Start with week 1, completing only the progress that matches your timeline. Therefore, if you start in the third week of March, follow directives in the chapter for the first and second weeks of March.

- If you're starting during the second month of a season, begin with Week 1 of the prior month and work your way through until the season ends, transitioning into the following Earth month. For example, if you start in April, begin with the exercises for March (Week 1 through Week 4). Then, skip the exercises for April in Part Two and continue with May at the beginning of May.

- In a situation, where there are more than four weeks in a month, repeat the exercises for week 4, allowing for two weeks of practice.

- The activities build in intensity, therefore feel free to stay at any week's level. For example, you might be feeling really good doing week one's activities and decide to continue that for the entire month, never actually moving forward to weeks two, three, or four. The beauty of the natural growth cycle is that you can visit the other activities next year. It grows and evolves with you as you're ready.

- Hear me loudly when I say that there is no expectation for you to do everything in the pages of Part Two. Forcing yourself could do more harm, causing the burnout to progress rather than begin healing. This journey only works if you're willing to honor and respect yourself. Listen to what your body is telling you and know that the expectation is for you to work toward trusting it.

Everything else you need to know will be contained in Part Two once you find your starting phase. Remember the revelations you identified earlier. If the phase you are starting in came up on your chart, there is a chance that your start could be rocky with resistance. On the flip side, it also means you are beginning work in a phase that has the potential to materialize immediate and powerful shifts.

The Phase Calendar

December January	Winter	Water	Go to page 161
February	Transition	Earth	Go to page 181
March April	Spring	Wood	Go to page 75
May	Transition	Earth	Go to page 91
June July	Summer	Fire	Go to page 102
August	Transition	Earth	Go to page 121
September October	Fall	Metal	Go to page 133
November	Transition	Earth	Go to page 147

BREATHE.

TAKE THE NEXT STEP WHEN YOU ARE READY.

Part Two

The Wood Phase
Spring Season

Wood feeds the flame of purpose,

its strength drawn from deep roots.

It holds firm in the earth,

grounded, unyielding,

a quiet power that endures.

Wood is the element that fuels our ability to dream. In Classical Oriental Medicine, the Wood Element is linked to physical, emotional, mental, and spiritual aspects of ourselves. It is necessary that we explore all of these aspects to establish balance and harmony in this elemental phase that serves as the foundation for the next season of Summer. As we move through these two months, you'll be invited to explore your active Wood-driven energetic imbalances as well as learn what is accessible when they are released.

Wood is responsible to ensure that our energy is free and easily wandering throughout the body. While this might bring forth imagery of wanderlust, what it truly reflects is the fluidity and flow we need to obtain harmony. Balance achieved will never be a constant 50/50; instead, we should aim for a constant flow between 49 and 51. The smooth transition between the two polarities of life allows for efficient use of energy that translates into what can be described as a fairly consistent state of peace.

In this season, you'll be prompted with an active action on odd-numbered weeks and then given the space for reflection and healing on the even-numbered weeks. As with all the phases, the exercises will progress in intensity as the weeks go on. Honor yourself, by giving yourself permission to pause or modify the work. Feel free to linger at a particular week with no guilt for not moving forward to completing every exercise. This journey is not about perfect, it is about progress at a pace that is sustainable.

Before we get started, let's first take a moment and pulse check your active Wood Phase Imbalances by completing the portion of the Burnout Assessment strictly focused on this elemental phase. Use this time to check-in to increase your awareness of the energetic imbalances associated with this phase. It should be expected that current imbalances will become exaggerated during this timeframe, this might mean that new imbalances may even present themselves.

Check-In

For each symptom listed, check the box if the symptom is present now or if you've encountered it within the past two weeks.

Physical Wood Phase Imbalances:

- ○ Hypertension (including labile blood pressure)
- ○ Oily skin/hair
- ○ Boils
- ○ Muscle cramps in limbs
- ○ Vertigo
- ○ Hearing issues (including ringing in ears)
- ○ Spasmodic constipation
- ○ Sciatic pain
- ○ Pain in ribs
- ○ Heartburn
- ○ Swallowing difficulties
- ○ Eye and ear pain
- ○ Shingles
- ○ Increased clumsiness and susceptibility to accidents
- ○ Nail conditions (including dry, brittle, and thick nails)
- ○ Breast pain
- ○ Tendon conditions (including injuries and tendonitis)
- ○ Hypoglycemia
- ○ Blurry vision
- ○ Sensitivity to light and sound
- ○ Urinary tract issues (including cystitis, urethritis)
- ○ Itchiness in eyes and genital/anal areas

- ○ Joint and muscle conditions (including lax joints and tense muscles)
- ○ Irritable bowel syndrome
- ○ Chronic neck and shoulder tension
- ○ Headaches (including occipital and lateral)
- ○ Migraines
- ○ Jaw joint dysfunction (TMJ syndrome)
- ○ Facial nerve pain
- ○ Peripheral neuropathy
- ○ Sexual dysfunction
- ○ Menstrual issues (including painful cycles and PMS)
- ○ Substance abuse

Score:

Potential Energetic Wood Phase Imbalances:

- ○ Intense and forceful behavior: You often exhibit behavior that is aggressive or overly assertive, which can be overwhelming to others.
- ○ Lack of restraint: You find it difficult to control your impulses or refrain from acting on your immediate desires.
- ○ Difficulty in fair interactions: You struggle to engage in interactions that require fairness and equity, often prioritizing your own needs or views.
- ○ Challenges in collaboration: Working with others is difficult for you, especially when it involves compromising or sharing responsibilities.
- ○ Discomfort with uncertainty: You feel uneasy or anxious in situations where outcomes are uncertain or unknown.
- ○ Hostile behavior: You may frequently behave in a hostile manner, which can include being verbally or physically confrontational.

- ○ Overbearing attitudes: Your demeanor can be excessively controlling or demanding, often trying to impose your will on others.
- ○ Unpredictable or poorly considered actions: You tend to act without thinking things through, leading to unpredictable or rash decisions.
- ○ Inconsistent decision-making: Your decision-making process often lacks consistency, changing based on mood or external pressures.
- ○ Oppositional behavior: You regularly exhibit resistance or opposition in situations where cooperation is expected.
- ○ Domineering interactions: In your interactions with others, you tend to dominate the conversation or situation, often at the expense of others' participation.
- ○ Easily irritated behavior: You are quick to become irritated or annoyed, often over seemingly minor issues.

Score:

Remember, any of the imbalances you checked are simply your body's way of communicating with you that something is out of alignment. The exercises for this phase will help to restore alignment by releasing what might be causing your energy to stagnate as well as providing nourishment in areas where you've possibly depleted your energetic reserves.

Now you're ready to begin with your first exercise. The way you approach the next pages is completely up to you. However, the chart below will give you a recommendation based off your burnout level score.

- **Stages 1-2**: Follow the structured plan in the book, introducing one new exercise per week.
- **Stages 3-4**: Move to a new exercise only if you have the capacity. Otherwise, repeat the prior exercise or take a pause to rest.
- **Stage 5**: Focus only on the first exercise of the phase. Reflect deeply and discuss your experience with a mental health practitioner.

March

Week 1

The following is an excerpt from the book *A New Earth* by Eckhart Tolle:

> "I mentioned my observation that after two ducks get into a fight, which never lasts long, they will separate and float off in opposite directions. Then each duck will flap its wings vigorously a few times, thus releasing the surplus energy that built up during the fight. After they flap their wings, they float on peacefully, as if nothing had ever happened.
>
> If the duck had a human mind, it would keep the fight alive by thinking, by story-making. As far as the body is concerned, the fight is still continuing, and the energy it generates in response to all those thoughts is emotion, which in turn generates more thinking. But this is how most humans live all the time. No situation or event is ever really finished. The mind and the mind-made 'me and my story' keep it going."

For this week, let's take some wisdom from the ducks using movement to release the surplus stagnated Wood energy.

I want you to find a way to move intentionally every day and aim for 10-22 minutes of releasing movement. This could be a walk outside, a kitchen dance party, kickboxing, spring cleaning, or even Qigong.

If you'd like to try Qigong for this week, I've designed a special 22-minute flow for you. Access this video resource at: **www.HRartInstitute.com**.

Week 2

This week, continue your practice of daily releasing movements. Hopefully, you've found something that feels genuinely good and you find your body naturally craving it.

Before moving into this week's prompt, take a moment and check in regarding last week's action item. You want to ensure that the movement you've gravitated toward felt releasing, meaning you felt lighter upon completion, even if it was only a tad bit lighter. If you are participating in a movement that left you feeling even more tired than when you started, it's probably not a great match. For example, if you pursued my recommendation for spring cleaning, if this was more like an excuse to do a household chore rather than intentional movement toward the work we are doing together, then it makes sense why it wouldn't hit the mark.

If this is the case for you, continue seeking out that releasing movement for yourself. If you found it, continue engaging in it.

Now this week for your reflection, focus on Eckhart Tolle's words directed toward how humans typically hold anger through the act of stories, ruminating on a situation rather than releasing it.

Get your journal and free-write the following prompts. Write for no longer than 4 minutes per prompt and make sure you at least linger at each for 1 minute. I know you're wondering, and the answer is yes—use a timer. These are not just recommended time frames. I want them in practice. This ensures that you give each prompt a fair shake while also not falling into the unproductive pit of venting.

Reflection Prompts:

1. What anger or frustration stories are you actively ruminating on?
2. What anger or frustration stories have you been chronically feeding?

Week 3

You've now experienced releasing the stagnated energy through movement, but now we want to engage in an exercise that will encourage inner movement. This specific exercise will target the Wood Element and stagnated emotional and mental thought patterns around anger and frustration. To do this we will engage in the following breathwork exercise daily.

If you'd prefer to practice this exercise through a guided audio, I've created one for you. You can access it at: www.hrartinstitute.com.

1. Begin by focusing on your natural breath, tuning into your natural rhythm of the inhale and exhale.

2. Continue with your natural breathing rhythm but guide your inhale down to the belly. When you exhale, empty the belly. Continue this pattern until it is comfortable. It is not necessary to attempt to deepen or elongate the breathing rhythm. You may do so if this happens naturally as the body relaxes, otherwise, stay with the rhythm that is comfortable for you. At no time, should you feel like you are without an adequate amount of breath.

3. Begin incorporating a visual with your inhale. Imagine that the breath is now an emerald green mist. Inhale this mist into your body. Send this emerald green mist into your liver and gallbladder.

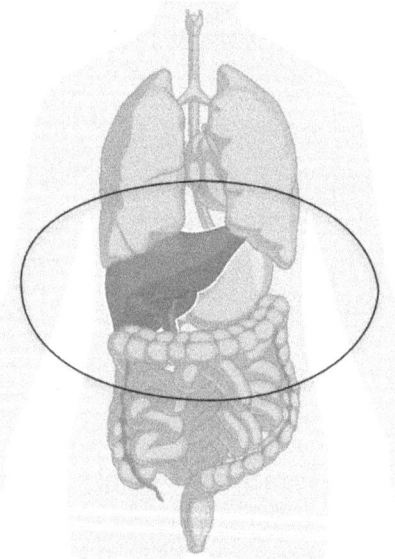

4. Now start exhaling out through the mouth while hearing in your mind or audibly making a *Shoooo* sound. Imagine this sound vibrating the liver and gallbladder, releasing stagnated emotional and mental energies. See these energies being carried out of the body by the breath on the exhale.

5. Complete 8 repetitions of inhaling the color and exhaling the sound audibly or inaudibly.

Week 4

This week's reflection will be driven by observation. It is said that the actual seasonal change to Spring in our environment is what makes these Wood imbalances more pronounced.

Individuals with excessive Wood energy will be aggravated by the seasonal change and tend to become consumed by anger and irritability. While individuals with depleted Wood energy can find themselves withdrawing and fearful.

This week I want you to tune in and observe how the season is impacting you. What do you notice coming to the surface? What themes are presenting themselves time and time again? Log these in your journal, recognizing that they possess hints of what truly needs healing to nurture your Wood Phase.

April

Week 1

The Spring season signals a pretty significant change in our energetic nourishment from food. During this season, you may have noticed an innate appreciation for the vibrant green of plants and trees sprouting. These plants call us outside, but they also invite us to partake for additional energetic nutrients through food.

Our bodies naturally begin to ask for dark leafy greens, like kale, collards, chicory, spinach, rocket, mustard, bok choi, chard, endive, coriander, parsley, and even green tops of vegetables.

This week I want you to try some dark leafy greens. I've included some of my favorite ways to add these greens at: **www.HRartInstitute.com**.

We're aiming for maybe 2-3 meals this week, where the dark leafy green is the star. Keep in mind that excess consumption could cause further Wood Phase imbalances. Therefore, this invitation is not insinuating that you overindulge in green smoothies, or limit your diet to strictly dark leafy green salads. In fact, if this is your current dietary practice, then use this week to focus on backing off the leafy greens and incorporating other foods.

Week 2

Before moving into this week's prompt, take a moment and check in regarding last week's action item. What did you observe about yourself? Did you have resistance to the dark leafy greens or the idea of restricting them? How did they make you feel, before, after, and while you were eating them? Capture your thoughts in your journal.

This week's reflection is going to be around food as a coping strategy for Wood Imbalances. Predominantly these coping strategies are in the form of highly processed foods (especially fast foods) and alcohol. They have a numbing effect on the liver which is the organ that manages the emotions and thoughts patterns of the Wood Element.

This week I want you to take some time exploring your why behind indulging in either highly processed foods or alcohol. Are you truly hungry when eating them? Is it an effort to stop a thought process or feeling? Does the indulging experience bring genuine joy?

This week isn't about saying you can't have this or that, but instead inviting you to be mindful before deciding to partake. Just as the dark leafy green contains energetic nutrients, highly processed foods and alcohol have their share of energetic impact as well. While we typically can manage when partaking on the occasional celebration or hard day, when it becomes a chronic coping tactic, our Wood Phase struggles.

Week 3

The Wood Element is known to have a connection to our eyes, physically and spiritually. As someone who has had prescription glasses for less than a decade, I've often wondered if my constant neglect of my Wood Element caused the development of stigmatism.

This week we won't be focusing on your physical vision capacity, but more on your spiritual vision capacity. Spiritual—meaning your ability to be connected to something larger than yourself. Vision is essential for this because it allows you to actually see what's possible.

However, in today's world there are many variables at play that impact your ability for a true vision. This is a Vision that is not tainted by external factors. It is connected to the core aspects of you that might actively be buried under multiple layers.

These layers can be fed through physical vision. This week I want you to experiment with what you expose yourself to from a physical vision standpoint–this includes anything you can see on a daily basis. What are you taking in regularly?

Use your journal as an observation log to take stock of the following sources:

1. Your physical environment: at work, at home, and any other common places you find yourself

2. Your media exposure: TV, images including social media, movies
3. Relational interactions: who you are around on a regular basis, their common interactions and mannerisms

Week 4

Last week you spent time evaluating and being curious about what you're actively exposing yourself to from a physical vision standpoint. This week, I want you to play with intentional physical vision and measure the impact.

To do this, pick one of the intentional vision sources from below:

1. Find a social media influencer or account that provides images that express what you hope to attain and experience in this life. Spend time exploring that channel or influencer's content throughout the week.
2. Select and watch a movie, TV show, documentary, or docu-series that resonates with a hope you have for your future self or the future world.
3. Create a vision board of images that inspire love, kindness, benevolence, compassion, and generosity within yourself. Provide the space and time to engage in this creative process.

After completing your engagement with your selected source, take some time to journal the impact. What did you notice about yourself as you were engaging and after you'd finished? Think in terms of answering one or all of the following prompts:

- What were you thinking about?
- How were you feeling?
- What did you find yourself wanting?
- What did you find yourself needing?

Check-In

Before moving on, let's take a minute and check in on our physical and energetic Wood Phase Imbalances. This is not an evaluation of how you did during these last two months, but rather a pulse check to acknowledge and know for our future work together.

For each symptom listed, check the box if the symptom is present now or if you've encountered it within the past two weeks.

Potential Physical Wood Phase Imbalances:

- ○ Hypertension (including labile blood pressure)
- ○ Oily skin/hair
- ○ Boils
- ○ Muscle cramps in limbs
- ○ Vertigo
- ○ Hearing issues (including ringing in ears)
- ○ Spasmodic constipation
- ○ Sciatic pain
- ○ Pain in ribs
- ○ Heartburn
- ○ Swallowing difficulties
- ○ Eye and ear pain
- ○ Shingles
- ○ Increased clumsiness and susceptibility to accidents
- ○ Nail conditions (including dry, brittle, and thick nails)
- ○ Breast pain
- ○ Tendon conditions (including injuries and tendonitis)
- ○ Hypoglycemia

- ○ Blurry vision
- ○ Sensitivity to light and sound
- ○ Urinary tract issues (including cystitis, urethritis)
- ○ Itchiness in eyes and genital/anal areas
- ○ Joint and muscle conditions (including lax joints and tense muscles)
- ○ Irritable bowel syndrome
- ○ Chronic neck and shoulder tension
- ○ Headaches (including occipital and lateral)
- ○ Migraines
- ○ Jaw joint dysfunction (TMJ syndrome)
- ○ Facial nerve pain
- ○ Peripheral neuropathy
- ○ Sexual dysfunction
- ○ Menstrual issues (including painful cycles and PMS)
- ○ Substance abuse

Score:

Energetic Wood Phase Imbalances:

- ○ Intense and forceful behavior: You often exhibit behavior that is aggressive or overly assertive, which can be overwhelming to others.
- ○ Lack of restraint: You find it difficult to control your impulses or refrain from acting on your immediate desires.
- ○ Difficulty in fair interactions: You struggle to engage in interactions that require fairness and equity, often prioritizing your own needs or views.
- ○ Challenges in collaboration: Working with others is difficult for you, especially when it involves compromising or sharing responsibilities.

- ○ Discomfort with uncertainty: You feel uneasy or anxious in situations where outcomes are uncertain or unknown.
- ○ Hostile behavior: You may frequently behave in a hostile manner, which can include being verbally or physically confrontational.
- ○ Overbearing attitudes: Your demeanor can be excessively controlling or demanding, often trying to impose your will on others.
- ○ Unpredictable or poorly considered actions: You tend to act without thinking things through, leading to unpredictable or rash decisions.
- ○ Inconsistent decision-making: Your decision-making process often lacks consistency, changing based on mood or external pressures.
- ○ Oppositional behavior: You regularly exhibit resistance or opposition in situations where cooperation is expected.
- ○ Domineering interactions: In your interactions with others, you tend to dominate the conversation or situation, often at the expense of others' participation.
- ○ Easily irritated behavior: You are quick to become irritated or annoyed, often over seemingly minor issues.

Score:

THE WORK
WILL STILL
BE THERE
TOMORROW.

The Earth Phase
Supporting Wood into Fire

In the stillness of Earth,
creativity finds its breath.
A fertile ground, steady and true,
where roots give rise to flames.
Here, the heart's fire is sparked,
lit by the freedom of flowing dreams.

When the Wood Phase is balanced, we will enter this seasonal transition to Earth filled with clarity about our path forward. However, when our Wood is imbalanced, we often experience a Spring season filled with aggressive energy that leaves us more frustrated and angrier at the world around us. These strong emotions are the body's attempts to shine light on areas of your life that need attention.

Particularly as you enter this seasonal transition period, the areas that are being exposed focus on what you need to pursue the path of your Heart's desires. The Heart is beginning to position itself into full focus as Summer is on the horizon.

The positive emotional attributes that accompany the Earth Phase become especially relevant at this time. These attributes include the ability to trust yourself, accept support, and be open to sympathy. This Phase is all about establishing a foundation for you to have what you need to move forward.

During this month, you'll be prompted to practice cultivating Earth energy in hopes to have it readily available for you as you advocate for your personal needs throughout the month. You'll also be given the space for reflection each week, to take stock on what the aggressive emotional aftermath of Spring might have to share with you. Before you get started, let's first take a moment for a pulse check on what active Earth Phase Imbalances you may be experiencing.

Check-In

For each symptom listed, check the box if the symptom is present now or if you've encountered it within the past two weeks.

Potential Physical Earth Phase Imbalances:

- ○ Muscular and lymphatic dysfunction
- ○ Venous disorders
- ○ Digestive and appetite issues
- ○ Weight management difficulties
- ○ Fluid and secretion management issues
- ○ Tissue swelling and gland issues
- ○ General discomfort and pain
- ○ Reproductive and abdominal dysfunctions
- ○ Blood and vascular health issues
- ○ Eye and oral health issues
- ○ Swelling of internal organs

Score:

Potential Energetic Earth Phase Imbalances:

- ○ Challenges with change and orientation: You find it difficult to adapt to new situations or changes in your environment, often feeling disoriented when your routine is disrupted.
- ○ Excessive caregiving or controlling behavior: You may engage in overly protective or controlling behaviors, often putting the needs of others before your own to an unhealthy extent.

- Indecision and uncertainty: You frequently struggle to make decisions, feeling uncertain even when faced with relatively simple choices.

- Self-identity and autonomy issues: You have difficulties maintaining a strong sense of self and often rely on others for validation or direction.

- Focus and thought organization difficulties: You find it challenging to maintain focus or organize your thoughts effectively, which can interfere with completing tasks.

- Dependency and pleasing behavior: You tend to depend too much on others for emotional support or approval and often act primarily to please others at your own expense.

- Unstable thought and decision-making processes: Your thoughts and decisions may frequently change, lacking consistency and often appear erratic or poorly planned.

- Emotional dependence and exaggerated affection: You exhibit a strong emotional attachment to others, often showing affection to an excessive degree that might not be reciprocated or appropriate.

- Inability to progress or stabilize: You often feel stuck, unable to move forward or find stability in various aspects of your life, from relationships to career.

- Interference in personal affairs: You may intrude into the personal matters of others, offering unsolicited advice or assistance, and overstepping boundaries.

- Low energy and depressive states: You frequently experience periods of low energy and feelings of sadness or hopelessness that affect your daily functioning.

- Invasion of personal space and boundaries: You might struggle with respecting the personal space and boundaries of others, often invading their physical or emotional space unintentionally.

- Excessive worrying and conformity: You tend to worry excessively about various aspects of life and may conform to others'

expectations or societal norms without true alignment with your own desires or beliefs.

Score:

Remember, any of the imbalances you checked are simply your body's way of communicating with you that something is out of alignment. The exercises for this phase will help to restore alignment by releasing what might be causing your energy to stagnate as well as providing nourishment in areas where you've possibly depleted your energetic reserves.

Now you're ready to begin with your first exercise. The way you approach the next pages is completely up to you. However, the chart below will give you a recommendation based off your burnout level score.

- **Stages 1-2**: Follow the structured plan in the book, introducing one new exercise per week.

- **Stages 3-4**: Move to a new exercise only if you have the capacity. Otherwise, repeat the prior exercise or take a pause to rest.

- **Stage 5**: Focus only on the first exercise of the phase. Reflect deeply and discuss your experience with a mental health practitioner.

May

Weeks 1 + 3

For this month, your breathwork practice during weeks 1 and 3 will be the same. That way you can really focus on the benefits of the practice rather than losing valuable time trying to learn new mechanics of another exercise.

This breathwork is designed to bring Earth energy into your body. I highly recommend that you complete this exercise daily and even continue it on the even weeks while doing the reflective prompts. After your breathwork practice, make sure to journal and log anything that surfaced or things that you experienced. If you'd prefer to practice this exercise through a guided audio, you can access it at: www.HRartInstitute.com.

1. Begin seated in a chair, with your feet flat on the floor. Take a moment and really focus on feeling your feet connect to the surface beneath you.

2. Imagine your feet becoming one with the surface beneath you, think ice cream melting on a warm sidewalk.

3. Now start focusing on your natural breath, tuning into your natural rhythm of the inhale and exhale.

4. Continue with your natural breathing rhythm, but guide your inhale down to the belly. When you exhale, empty the belly. Continue this pattern until it is comfortable. It is not necessary to attempt to deepen or elongate the breathing rhythm. You may do so if this happens naturally as the body relaxes, otherwise, stay with the rhythm that is comfortable for you. At no time, should you feel like you are without an adequate amount of breath.

5. Now imagine tree roots growing from your feet and extending into the Earth.

6. On your next inhale imagine these tree roots activating and beginning to absorb Earth energy. Inhale and bring this energy up the tree roots into your feet, up your legs, up your spine.
7. When it arrives at the top of your head, exhale it down the front of your body and allow it to pool and overfill your lower abdomen.
8. Continue absorbing and filling yourself with Earth energy until the lower abdomen is overflowing.
9. Then place your hands one on top of the other on your lower abdomen and imagine the energy settling.
10. Slowly bring your attention back to the space you're in.

Week 2

This week, we are going to hit the pause button and take a look at the anger you've been experiencing. Each day this week, I want you to observe when you experience anger. What do you find yourself dwelling on? This could be someone or something they did. When you identify a source of anger, I want you to get your journal and free-write, why. Why do you have a right to be angry?

For this reflection exercise, I want you to actively engage in the art of venting. This is different from any other exercise you will find in this book, because for this emotional release we need the vent vomit.

Don't worry if you find yourself logging and venting on the same experience or individuals each day. Even if you pick different individuals and circumstances, it is not uncommon to realize that there is a link or theme embedded throughout them. Our anger is not caused by one season of life, but is often deeply rooted and intricately connected to many other seasons of this lifetime and previous.

Week 4

For this week's reflection, we will be revisiting your vent vomit from week 2. Our goal is to identify some wisdom from these experiences. The beauty of this Earth phase is that it possesses the ability to sort through your experiences to determine what is worthy of your energy and what is not.

However, to do so requires you to trust yourself. Hopefully you've been doing your breathwork and actively cultivating Earth energy for this moment.

Each day, read one of your previous entries out loud, slowly, just to yourself. As you read, listen to what is unsaid between the words. Pay attention to what rises up within you. Where does your mind wander? How do you feel? What do you feel?

Log it all down in your journal. Then ask yourself one final question: Is there anything I need to do right now with this information? If the answer is yes, then write that down and make a plan to take action. If the answer is no, trust that the increased awareness was sufficient for your development, growth, and healing at this time.

Check-In

Before moving on, let's take a minute to check on our physical and energetic Earth Phase Imbalances. This is not an evaluation of how you did during the last month, but rather a pulse check to acknowledge and know for your future work.

For each symptom listed, check the box if the symptom is present now or if you've encountered it within the past two weeks.

Potential Physical Earth Phase Imbalances:

- ○ Muscular and lymphatic dysfunction
- ○ Venous disorders
- ○ Digestive and appetite issues
- ○ Weight management difficulties
- ○ Fluid and secretion management issues
- ○ Tissue swelling and gland issues
- ○ General discomfort and pain
- ○ Reproductive and abdominal dysfunctions
- ○ Blood and vascular health issues
- ○ Eye and oral health issues
- ○ Swelling of internal organs

Score:

Potential Energetic Earth Phase Imbalances:

- ○ Challenges with change and orientation: You find it difficult to adapt to new situations or changes in your environment, often feeling disoriented when your routine is disrupted.

- ○ Excessive caregiving or controlling behavior: You may engage in overly protective or controlling behaviors, often putting the needs of others before your own to an unhealthy extent.
- ○ Indecision and uncertainty: You frequently struggle to make decisions, feeling uncertain even when faced with relatively simple choices.
- ○ Self-identity and autonomy issues: You have difficulties maintaining a strong sense of self and often rely on others for validation or direction.
- ○ Focus and thought organization difficulties: You find it challenging to maintain focus or organize your thoughts effectively, which can interfere with completing tasks.
- ○ Dependency and pleasing behavior: You tend to depend too much on others for emotional support or approval and often act primarily to please others at your own expense.
- ○ Unstable thought and decision-making processes: Your thoughts and decisions may frequently change, lacking consistency and often appear erratic or poorly planned.
- ○ Emotional dependence and exaggerated affection: You exhibit a strong emotional attachment to others, often showing affection to an excessive degree that might not be reciprocated or appropriate.
- ○ Inability to progress or stabilize: You often feel stuck, unable to move forward or find stability in various aspects of your life, from relationships to career.
- ○ Interference in personal affairs: You may intrude into the personal matters of others, offering unsolicited advice or assistance, and overstepping boundaries.
- ○ Low energy and depressive states: You frequently experience periods of low energy and feelings of sadness or hopelessness that affect your daily functioning.
- ○ Invasion of personal space and boundaries: You might struggle with respecting the personal space and boundaries of others, often invading their physical or emotional space unintentionally.

○ Excessive worrying and conformity: You tend to worry excessively about various aspects of life and may conform to others' expectations or societal norms without true alignment with your own desires or beliefs.

Score:

The Fire Phase
Summer Season

Fire blazes like molten lava, fueled by the heart's desire.
When it cools, we turn inward, waiting for the next spark—
the one worthy of igniting our next blaze.
Fire shapes the details of our dreams,
transforming vision into reality, one flame at a time.

The Fire Element and its corresponding season of Summer make up the most yang time of year. It's a little bit of a contradiction given that we commonly associate Summer with vacation, a time of relaxation and rejuvenation to prepare for the busy Fall season. However, this time of year is intended to be the most productive. During Summer, you are meant to be highly active. This is when you can make big moves to truly begin to materialize desires of the Heart.

The Heart is the organ that is physically associated with the Fire Phase, however it is also represented from a psychospiritual component. Speaking of the Heart as the deepest truest part of yourself, it represents the cumulative work of everything you are and everything you are becoming. It's the place where you transform logic, data, and experience into lessons that evolve who you are as an individual.

In this season, you won't be prompted to do any real deep work but rather to focus on action. Therefore, every week you'll be given challenges to take action. Before we get started let's first take a pulse check on what active Fire Phase Imbalances you may be experiencing.

Check-In

For each symptom listed, check the box if the symptom is present now or if you've encountered it within the past two weeks.

Potential Physical Fire Phase Imbalances:

- ○ Sleep disturbances
- ○ Heart conditions
- ○ Irregular heart functions
- ○ Circulatory system disorders
- ○ Facial complexion changes
- ○ Heat regulation issues
- ○ Sexual response issues
- ○ Skin conditions
- ○ Pulmonary hypertension
- ○ Painful urination
- ○ Anemia
- ○ Speech and sensation disturbances
- ○ Chest pain

Score:

Potential Energetic Fire Phase Imbalances:

- ○ Boundary issues: You often have difficulty setting and maintaining personal boundaries, which might lead to feeling overwhelmed or taken advantage of by others.

- Pacing and stimulation management: You find it challenging to manage and maintain a comfortable pace in activities, often feeling either overstimulated or understimulated.
- Anxiety about the unknown: You experience significant anxiety when faced with uncertain situations or future outcomes that are not clear.
- Sleep disturbances: You frequently have trouble either falling asleep or staying asleep, which impacts your overall health and well-being.
- Expression difficulties: You struggle to clearly express your thoughts and feelings, which can lead to misunderstandings or a sense of isolation.
- Heightened startle response: You are easily startled by unexpected sounds or movements, more so than others.
- Cognitive imbalances: You experience difficulties in your thought processes, which can manifest as disorganized thinking or difficulty concentrating.
- Hypersensitivity: You are extremely sensitive to physical sensations, emotions, or social interactions, often feeling overwhelmed by them.
- Social flirtation and seduction: You tend to engage frequently in flirtatious or seductive behavior, which may affect your social interactions.
- Elevated emotional responses: Your emotional reactions are often more intense than the situation warrants, which can be draining for you and those around you.
- Overly positive outlook: You maintain an excessively optimistic view, even in situations where such optimism may not be warranted.
- Intense emotional feelings toward others: You often feel deep and overwhelming emotions toward others, which can affect your personal relationships.

- ○ Difficulty with emotional or physical detachment: You find it hard to detach yourself from situations or relationships, even when they are harmful or unfulfilling.
- ○ Excessive talking: You tend to talk more than most people, often dominating conversations or speaking without thinking about the impact on others.
- ○ Naivety in trust: You often trust people too readily, which can lead to disappointment or exploitation.

Score:

Remember, any of the imbalances you checked are simply your body's way of communicating with you that something is out of alignment. The exercises for this phase will help to restore alignment by releasing what might be causing your energy to stagnate as well as providing nourishment in areas where you've possibly depleted your energetic reserves.

Now you're ready to begin with your first exercise. The way you approach the next pages is completely up to you. However, the chart below will give you a recommendation based off your burnout level score.

- **Stages 1-2**: Follow the structured plan in the book, introducing one new exercise per week.
- **Stages 3-4**: Move to a new exercise only if you have the capacity. Otherwise, repeat the prior exercise or take a pause to rest.
- **Stage 5**: Focus only on the first exercise of the phase. Reflect deeply and discuss your experience with a mental health practitioner.

June

Week 1

For the first 4 weeks of this season, we are going to focus on releasing built-up stagnated energy in your Fire elemental composition. This energy is typically stagnated in the Heart or Small Intestine Meridian.

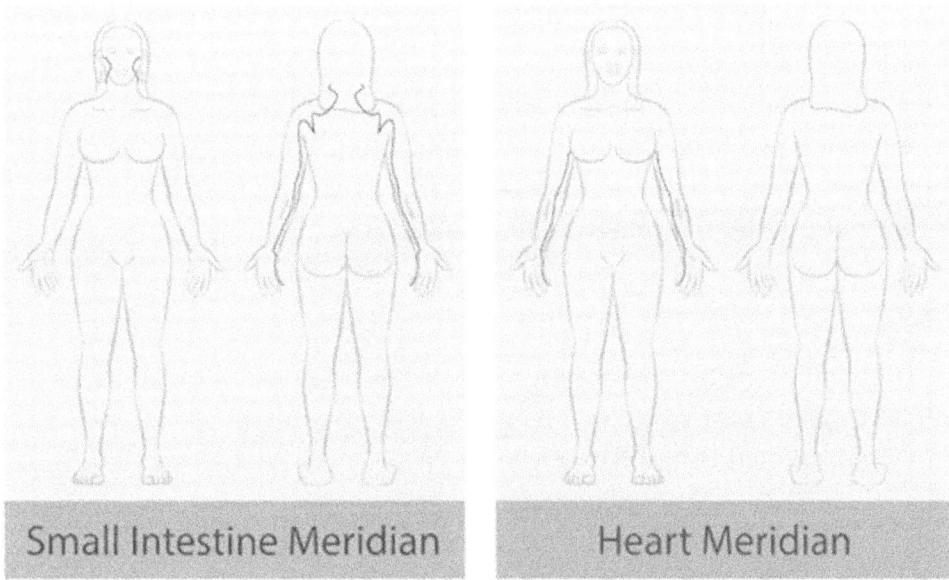

To ease you into these cleansing practices, we are going to begin with sound and vibration. In Medical Qigong, there is a practice known as Healing Sounds that is highly effective in moving stubborn energy at multiple levels. This practice uses breathwork, sound, visualization, and color. The sound that is associated with this element is the *Ha* sound, like *Ha Ha Ha*.

Therefore, every time you laugh, stagnated Fire energy is potentially being moved. You could even make the argument that laughter is the body's way of trying to move that energy... which provides clarity as to why some individuals laugh at perceived inappropriate times.

This week your task is to laugh as much as you can. I also want you to get in the habit of doing mini-reflections. Check in before and after your laughing sessions to see if you notice any differences or developments.

For your laughing sessions, you have so many options, but here are a few ideas:

- Dive into an old comedy sitcom that you can binge watch throughout the week.
- Schedule time with a friend that always makes you laugh.
- Find a new comedy and go to the movies or watch it at home.
- Get silly with your loved ones, play games, or do something playful in nature.

It doesn't matter what you do, but the goal is to have some sort of good genuine laughing time for at least 10 minutes a day. It doesn't have to happen all at once. There can be short bursts of laughter throughout the day that culminate in a total of 10 minutes.

Week 2

Now that you've spent a week laughing and moving energy with the organic healing sound, this week we are going to get a bit more intentional by having you make the sound.

Our intention for this week will be focused on caring for your physical body, specifically targeting those physical Fire imbalances you identified at the beginning of the season. In fact, I want you to think about those specific symptoms as you engage in this exercise. Imagine that you are doing this exercise to specifically address each symptom.

This exercise also requires you to engage in abdominal breathing. This is the breathing pattern where your inhale fills the abdominal cavity, and the exhale empties it.

If you'd like to practice this breathing technique before getting started with the exercise, I've created an abdominal breathing practice audio for you to follow. Access it at: **www.HRartInstitute.com**.

Physical Body Fire Release Exercise:

1. Begin abdominal breathing.
2. Imagine your inhaled breath becomes a beautiful ruby red vapor that comes into the body and fills your heart.
3. Breathe in the ruby red and continue filling your heart.
4. Start to incorporate the *Ha* healing sound on your exhale, making sure it is loud and short. It should feel like a pumping sensation to the heart. It should be a physical experience.
5. Once comfortable in the rhythm of seeing the color on the inhale and making the sound on the exhale, complete the exercise 9 times.

Try to complete this exercise at least 3 rounds this week. Make sure you capture your observations of how you feel before, during, and after in your journal.

If you'd prefer to have me guide you in an audio track through this exercise, you can access it at: **www.HRartInstitute.com**.

Week 3

This week we will be shifting our releasing intention to focus on mental and emotional stagnations. You might want to revisit your energetic Fire imbalances list to see what types of energy are specifically being targeted this week.

Your exercise will be very similar to last week, with only one change in the volume and length of the sound. This week instead of loud and short, you will use a normal speaking volume and allow the sound to be carried on the exhale.

Emotional/Mental Body Fire Release Exercise:

1. Begin abdominal breathing.
2. Imagine your inhaled breath becomes a beautiful ruby red vapor that comes into the body and fills your heart.
3. Breathe in the ruby red and continue filling your heart.
4. Start to incorporate the *Ha* healing sound on your exhale, using a normal speaking tone and holding it for the entire exhale. It should

be more like *Haaaaaaaaa,* and it should generate an internal vibration within the heart area.

5. Once comfortable in the rhythm of seeing the color on the inhale and making the sound on the exhale, complete the exercise 9 times.

Try to complete this exercise at least 3 rounds this week. Make sure you capture your observations of how you feel before, during, and after in your journal.

If you'd prefer to have me guide you in an audio track through this exercise, you can access it at: **www.HRartInstitute.com**.

Week 4

This week's intention will be spiritual. Think of spiritual as the purest version of yourself. It is the energetic vibration intertwined with your values, beliefs, and purpose. It is the depth we often are seeking when we engage in any self-help work looking for clarity around why we exist in this present time. It can be connected to faith but is not a requirement. I encourage you to think of this concept as your ability to connect to something bigger. It provides meaning to your actions. It inspires your desire for impact, influence, and legacy.

This week's exercise will be the same as last week's, with just a change to your volume. This week's volume to access the spiritual level is supersoft or inaudible. You can even play with making the sound in your mind and not physically doing it.

Spiritual Body Fire Release Exercise:

1. Begin abdominal breathing.

2. Imagine your inhaled breath becomes a beautiful ruby red vapor that comes into the body and fills your heart.

3. Breathe in the ruby red and continue filling your heart.

4. Start to incorporate the inaudible or super quiet *Ha* healing sound on your exhale. Turn your intention inward and focus on magnifying the vibration within each exhale. If it feels right, you can even make the sound on an exasperated sigh. This modification also becomes handy if you find yourself feeling an energy that is refusing to move.

5. Once comfortable in the rhythm of seeing the color on the inhale and making the sound on the exhale, complete the exercise 9 times.

Try to complete this exercise at least 3 rounds this week. Make sure you capture your observations of how you feel before, during, and after in your journal.

If you'd prefer to have me guide you in an audio track through this exercise, you can access it at: **www.HRartInstitute.com**.

July

Week 1

One of the common causes of imbalances during Summer is excess. Despite this being a time for action, we have a tendency to overdo it. We refer to this as an excess condition that moves us away from a state of balance. Therefore, I'd like to focus the final four weeks of this season on activities that allow you to focus on balance.

In Medical Qigong, we refer to these types of movement-based exercises as regulation exercises. Their intention is to do just that—regulate or balance our system. Each week you'll be introduced to a new movement that can be used to regulate your energetic system. These movements will be a great resource for you throughout the years for times when you experience excess or overwhelm, in other words, when you are stressed out and need to chill.

The first movement is called Pulling Down the Heavens. You can check out YouTube for a ton of Qigong teachers and their interpretations of the movement or you can watch the video practice I created for you. Access it at: **www.HRartInstitute.com**.

Pulling Down the Heavens Exercise:

1. Begin with your hands at your hips, with your palms facing the earth.

2. Stand with your feet about shoulder width apart and knees slightly engaged.

3. Connect with the earth and feel rooted, grounded, and firmly planted through your feet.

4. On your inhale, raise your hands on both sides until about chest high. Then flip your palms to face the sky. Feel the warmth of the sun on your palms.

5. Bring your palms toward each other over your head, then exhale bringing both hands down in front of the center of your body.

6. Imagine the energy being cycled through and rooted into your lower abdomen, which is an area we call the Lower Dantian. This is where we have a reservoir for energetic reserves.

7. Inhale and complete another sequence of steps 4-6, continuing for at least 10 minutes.

Try to do this movement for 10 minutes a day. Make sure to capture in your journal anything you notice before, during, and after your movement practice.

Week 2

This week's movement is called Water Wheel. Feel free to watch the video practice I created for you. You can access it at: **www.HRartInstitute.com**.

Water Wheel Exercise:

1. Stand with your feet about shoulder width apart and knees slightly engaged.

2. Place your hands in front of the lower abdomen with palms facing each other. Focus on feeling your reservoir of energetic reserves that resides in this area.

3. Inhale and imagine pushing that energy down from your lower abdomen under your perineum, and then inhale the energy up your spine toward the top of your head.

4. At the top of your head, exhale and allow the energy to fall down over your face, then over your chest and back to the lower abdomen.

5. Inhale and repeat steps 2-4. As you become comfortable with your breathing pattern and visualizing the energy, begin to move your hands to follow that energy. Allow your hands to come upward as the energy and breath travel up the spine, and then cycle the hands out and down as you exhale the energy down the front of the body.

6. Allow your upper body to be fluid in movement as you mimic this cycle with your hands.

Try to do this movement for 10 minutes a day. Make sure to capture in your journal anything you notice before, during, and after your movement practice.

Week 3

This week's movement is called Golden Ball. The exercise is a fairly popular Qigong movement, so you can check out YouTube for videos from other teachers or you can reference the video practice I created for you. Access it at: **www.HRartInstitute.com.**

Golden Ball Exercise:

1. Stand with your feet about shoulder width apart and knees slightly engaged.
2. Begin with your hands at your hips, with palms facing the earth.
3. Connect with the earth and feel rooted, grounded, and firmly planted through your feet.
4. Imagine that a golden river of energy begins to emerge from the earth until you are standing in it. The river is about waist high so your fingertips and palms can just graze the surface.
5. Reach into the river, bringing your palms together as if you are collecting and creating a golden ball of energy.
6. Lift that golden ball of energy out of the river until it is about chest high.
7. Imagine the golden ball growing bigger, allowing your hands to expand outward to accommodate the growth.
8. Imagine the golden ball growing smaller, allowing your hands to follow.
9. Pull the golden ball toward you, allowing your hands to guide it until you feel the warmth on your chest.
10. Use your hands to push the ball away, returning the golden ball to about arm's length away.
11. Allow your hands to guide the ball downward back to the river.

12. Then separate your palms when you get back to waist height to return the golden energy to the river.

13. Repeat the sequence of steps 5-11 for at least 10 minutes.

Try to do this movement for 10 minutes a day. Make sure to capture in your journal anything you notice before, and after your movement practice.

Week 4

Our final movement is called Sourcing the Yin and Yang, and it is my personal favorite regulation exercise because it captures the delicate balance between calm and chaos. It shows how easily we can lose control as well as the power of imperfection.

When it comes to movement for energetic care, there are a lot of what my teacher would call "bells and whistles." If you engaged in YouTube over the last few weeks you may have encountered these. These are micro movement add-ons that make a movement look cooler. Most Qigong movements are extremely quiescent because the movement and magic are happening within. It is for this reason that I have come to believe over the years that my students can be doing the same move effectively yet each look uniquely different in style and technique. It is this uniqueness that reiterates why this approach works. Yes, you're engaging in a general energetic movement form. However, that form is a loose structure for you to engage on a level that is intimately connected to what you need at this moment.

When teaching this final movement, I often hear commentary that it's like trying to tap your head and rub your tummy at the same time. The Sourcing the Yin and Yang movement asks you to connect to the earth and the sun, two of nature's pure energy sources. It then invites you to simultaneously cycle them through your body, so I can totally get the reference people often make.

If you find yourself having similar thoughts, I'd like you to let go of the perfection in the bells and whistles. Instead tune in internally and focus on the intention of the movement. Connect to earth, connect to the sun, and cycle these pure, powerful energies within.

Just like all the others I've created a video practice for you. You can access it at: **www.HRartInstitute.com**.

Sourcing Yin and Yang Exercise:

1. Stand with your feet about shoulder width apart and knees slightly engaged.

2. Begin with your hands at your hips, with palms facing the earth.

3. Connect with the earth and feel rooted, grounded, and firmly planted through your feet.

4. Then take your left hand and reach toward the sky, with your palm facing the sun.

5. Connect with the sun, feeling the warmth on your left palm.

6. Check in with your right palm still feeling connected and rooted to the earth.

7. Slowly begin to spiral both hands, allowing them to travel toward the center of the body. The left hand slowly travels downward and the right hand slowly travels upward. When the hands pass each other, the palms should be facing one another.

8. Once the left hand hits waist level, allow it to spiral out with palm facing upward, circling around, extending your arm out to the left side, focusing on gathering that beautiful warm sun energy again.

9. Simultaneously, when the right hand hits the top of the head, allow it to spiral out with the palm facing downward, circling around, extending the arm out to the right side, focusing on gathering earth energy.

10. Once both hands have completed their circular motion and have returned to their starting positions of steps 5 and 6, repeat step 7. Continue the sequence of steps 5-9 for 5 minutes.

11. After 5 minutes, pause and return to steps 5 and 6. Breathe into this pause, feeling connected to the sun and earth energy.

12. Then spiral both hands toward your body and allow them to travel as you did in step 7. Pause when the right hand is overhead, and the left is at your waist.

13. Allow your right palm to reach toward the sun, connecting and feeling the warmth on your right palm.
14. Allow your left palm to face the earth and feel connected and rooted.
15. When ready, begin the cycling sequence again, but with the right palm traveling downward and the left palm traveling upward.
16. Repeat this sequence for another 5 minutes.
17. Afterward, place your hands in front of the lower abdomen with palms facing each other. Focus on feeling your reservoir of energetic reserves that resides in this area. Send your intention to settle the energy that you were actively cycling throughout this practice.

Try to do this movement for 10 minutes a day. Make sure to capture in your journal anything you notice before, during, and after your movement practice.

Check-In

Before moving on, let's take a minute to check on your physical and energetic Fire Phase Imbalances. This is not an evaluation of how you did during these last two months, but rather a pulse check to acknowledge and know for your future work.

For each symptom listed, check the box if the symptom is present now or if you've encountered it within the past two weeks.

Potential Physical Fire Phase Imbalances:

- ○ Sleep disturbances
- ○ Heart conditions
- ○ Irregular heart functions
- ○ Circulatory system disorders
- ○ Facial complexion changes

- ○ Heat regulation issues
- ○ Sexual response issues
- ○ Skin conditions
- ○ Pulmonary hypertension
- ○ Painful urination
- ○ Anemia
- ○ Speech and sensation disturbances
- ○ Chest pain

Score:

Potential Energetic Fire Phase Imbalances:

- ○ Boundary issues: You often have difficulty setting and maintaining personal boundaries, which might lead to feeling overwhelmed or taken advantage of by others.
- ○ Pacing and stimulation management: You find it challenging to manage and maintain a comfortable pace in activities, often feeling either overstimulated or understimulated.
- ○ Anxiety about the unknown: You experience significant anxiety when faced with uncertain situations or future outcomes that are not clear.
- ○ Sleep disturbances: You frequently have trouble either falling asleep or staying asleep, which impacts your overall health and well-being.
- ○ Expression difficulties: You struggle to clearly express your thoughts and feelings, which can lead to misunderstandings or a sense of isolation.
- ○ Heightened startle response: You are easily startled by unexpected sounds or movements, more so than others.

- ○ Cognitive imbalances: You experience difficulties in your thought processes, which can manifest as disorganized thinking or difficulty concentrating.
- ○ Hypersensitivity: You are extremely sensitive to physical sensations, emotions, or social interactions, often feeling overwhelmed by them.
- ○ Social flirtation and seduction: You tend to engage frequently in flirtatious or seductive behavior, which may affect your social interactions.
- ○ Elevated emotional responses: Your emotional reactions are often more intense than the situation warrants, which can be draining for you and those around you.
- ○ Overly positive outlook: You maintain an excessively optimistic view, even in situations where such optimism may not be warranted.
- ○ Intense emotional feelings toward others: You often feel deep and overwhelming emotions toward others, which can affect your personal relationships.
- ○ Difficulty with emotional or physical detachment: You find it hard to detach yourself from situations or relationships, even when they are harmful or unfulfilling.
- ○ Excessive talking: You tend to talk more than most people, often dominating conversations or speaking without thinking about the impact on others.
- ○ Naivety in trust: You often trust people too readily, which can lead to disappointment or exploitation.

Score:

YOUR
ENERGY
MATTERS

The Earth Phase
Supporting Fire into Metal

Earth steadies the heart's desire,

giving it space to take shape.

Here, the fire's passion cools,

refined into plans and precise actions,

ready to be forged into reality.

This seasonal transition comes after Summer, the most Yang time of year. Summer is a time filled with doing and Heart. The Fire Phase, when combined with the heat of the season, often leaves us exhausted. The shift back to a season that seeks a bit more Yin can feel unsettling. Also, the large contrast between the Heavens (sun, moon, and stars) energy associated with Fire, and the Earth energy associated with the Earth, can lead to feeling ungrounded as well as disconnected from your body.

We will use this time to settle the Yang energy and begin to regulate the Yin energy back through your system, with the ultimate goal of feeling a bit of inner peace and harmony as you approach Fall.

Fall and the Metal Phase will ask you to evaluate in preparation for the depths of reflection in Winter, giving even more reasons why you need to embrace this time to feel grounded and centered.

Each week this month, you'll be given a Medical Qigong exercise designed for regulation. Therefore, its focus is to cultivate harmony. Hopefully, after four weeks of different types of exercises, you'll be able to identify a few favorites that can become tools to utilize anytime you need a little harmony throughout the year.

Before we get started let's first take a pulse check on what active Earth Phase Imbalances you may be experiencing.

Check-In

For each symptom listed, check the box if the symptom is present now or if you've encountered it within the past two weeks.

Potential Physical Earth Phase Imbalances:

- ○ Muscular and lymphatic dysfunction
- ○ Venous disorders
- ○ Digestive and appetite issues
- ○ Weight management difficulties
- ○ Fluid and secretion management issues
- ○ Tissue swelling and gland issues
- ○ General discomfort and pain
- ○ Reproductive and abdominal dysfunctions
- ○ Blood and vascular health issues
- ○ Eye and oral health issues
- ○ Swelling of internal organs

Score:

Potential Energetic Earth Phase Imbalances:

- ○ Challenges with change and orientation: You find it difficult to adapt to new situations or changes in your environment, often feeling disoriented when your routine is disrupted.
- ○ Excessive caregiving or controlling behavior: You may engage in overly protective or controlling behaviors, often putting the needs of others before your own to an unhealthy extent.

- Indecision and uncertainty: You frequently struggle to make decisions, feeling uncertain even when faced with relatively simple choices.
- Self-identity and autonomy issues: You have difficulties maintaining a strong sense of self and often rely on others for validation or direction.
- Focus and thought organization difficulties: You find it challenging to maintain focus or organize your thoughts effectively, which can interfere with completing tasks.
- Dependency and pleasing behavior: You tend to depend too much on others for emotional support or approval and often act primarily to please others at your own expense.
- Unstable thought and decision-making processes: Your thoughts and decisions may frequently change, lacking consistency and often appear erratic or poorly planned.
- Emotional dependence and exaggerated affection: You exhibit a strong emotional attachment to others, often showing affection to an excessive degree that might not be reciprocated or appropriate.
- Inability to progress or stabilize: You often feel stuck, unable to move forward or find stability in various aspects of your life, from relationships to career.
- Interference in personal affairs: You may intrude into the personal matters of others, offering unsolicited advice or assistance, and overstepping boundaries.
- Low energy and depressive states: You frequently experience periods of low energy and feelings of sadness or hopelessness that affect your daily functioning.
- Invasion of personal space and boundaries: You might struggle with respecting the personal space and boundaries of others, often invading their physical or emotional space unintentionally.
- Excessive worrying and conformity: You tend to worry excessively about various aspects of life and may conform to others'

expectations or societal norms without true alignment with your own desires or beliefs.

Score:

Remember, any of the imbalances you checked are simply your body's way of communicating with you that something is out of alignment. The exercises for this phase will help to restore alignment by releasing what might be causing your energy to stagnate as well as providing nourishment in areas where you've possibly depleted your energetic reserves.

Now you're ready to begin with your first exercise. The way you approach the next pages is completely up to you. However, the chart below will give you a recommendation based off your burnout level score.

- **Stages 1-2**: Follow the structured plan in the book, introducing one new exercise per week.

- **Stages 3-4**: Move to a new exercise only if you have the capacity. Otherwise, repeat the prior exercise or take a pause to rest.

- **Stage 5**: Focus only on the first exercise of the phase. Reflect deeply and discuss your experience with a mental health practitioner.

August

Week 1

If you prefer to do this week's exercise following a video, you can access the one I've created for you at: **www.HRartInstitute.com**.

Exercise: Pulling Down the Heavens

1. Begin standing with your feet about shoulder width apart. Soften your knees by bending them. If you prefer, you can modify this exercise by doing it while seated in a chair. Just make sure your chair does not have arms and your feet are flat on the floor.
2. Extend your arms down in an upside down "V" shape, allowing your palms to face the Earth, and take a moment to feel the energy of the Earth.
3. Inhale and begin to raise your arms, extending along the sides of your body.
4. When you reach your chest, flip your palms so they face the sky. Take a moment to connect to the Heavens (sun, moon, and stars).
5. Continue extending your arms, with your palms facing the sky.
6. At about neck height, begin to bend your arms inward until they are over your head with the palms facing the top of your head.
7. Exhale and bring the arms downward, allowing both your hands to be about 2-3 inches apart, following the center of your body down, with palms facing the Earth.
8. When your hands reach the lower abdomen, repeat steps 2-7 for at least 9 rounds.

Internally, imagine that you are guiding Heaven and Earth energy throughout the body to balance and cultivate harmony. Allow any excess energy that is found to settle and store in the Lower Abdomen. It is recommended that you practice this exercise daily this week. Make sure you use your journal to log any experiences that you feel are worthy to capture.

Week 2

If you prefer to do this week's exercise following a video, you can access the one I've created for you at: **www.HRartInstitute.com**.

Exercise: Pulling Down the Heavens with Sound

This exercise will build upon the one from last week. While the movement and intention will be the same, this week we will incorporate a sound on the exhale while the hands are traveling down the front center of the body. This sound will vibrate the tissues and organs, freeing up other energy that needs to be circulated and ultimately settled.

The sound is *Sheeee*. Allow this sound to accompany your exhale as you complete the Pulling Down the Heavens Exercise. Keep your volume to a normal conversational level for 9 repetitions. Then drop your volume to a whisper, nearly inaudible, for 9 more repetitions.

It is recommended that you practice this sequence daily this week. Make sure you use your journal to log any experiences that you feel are worthy to capture.

Week 3

If you prefer to do this week's exercise following a video, you can access the one I've created for you at: **www.HRartInstitute.com**.

Exercise: Golden Ball

1. Begin standing with your feet about shoulder width apart. Soften your knees by bending them. If you prefer, you can modify this exercise by doing it while seated in a chair. Just make sure your chair does not have arms and your feet are flat on the floor.

2. Extend your arms down in an upside down "V" shape, allowing your palms to face the Earth. Take a moment to feel the energy of the Earth.

3. Imagine a Golden River of energy emerging from the Earth and bubbling up to about your waist. Allow your fingertips to glide over the surface of the imaginary river.
4. Now reach into the river and collect a ball of energy.
5. Imagine holding that ball of energy in your hands and raising it up out of the river until it's about chest high in front of your body.
6. Then expand your hands, allowing the ball to grow bigger.
7. Compress your hands, guiding the ball back to its original size.
8. Pull the ball into your chest, so you feel the energy lightly touch your skin.
9. Push the ball away, returning it back to its original position.
10. Then guide the ball back down to the river and disperse the energy.
11. Repeat steps 4-10, for at least 9 repetitions.

This exercise tunes you into the eight movements of energy. They are gathering, rising, expanding, contracting, pulling, pushing, falling, and dispersing. See if you can tune into the movement of energy that is the focus of each step.

It is recommended that you practice this exercise daily this week. Make sure you use your journal to log any experiences that you feel are worthy to capture.

Week 4

This final exercise is a visualization. All the movement will be facilitated internally by your mind. If you prefer to do this week's exercise following a guided audio, you can access the one I've created for you at: **www.HRartInstitute.com**.

Exercise: Microcosmic Orbit

1. Find a comfortable seat and take a moment to ground yourself. Feel connected to the ground beneath you, either through your feet or your spine.

2. Now begin turning inward by following the natural rhythm of your breath. Notice all the subtle details of the inhale and all the subtle details of the exhale.

3. Begin to focus your attention on your lower abdomen, tuning into the reservoir of energetic reserves that is stored there.

4. On the next inhale, imagine pushing that energy from the lower abdomen down between your legs past the perineum. Imagine it then begins to rise up the spine like a warm vapor.

5. When the vapor reaches the top of your head, begin to exhale, allowing the energy to fall down the front of your body. Imagine it coating the front of your body like a stream of warm oil.

6. When the warm oil reaches the lower abdomen, repeat step 4 and continue the sequence for at least 9 orbits.

This visualization is all about guiding an internal orbit that allows wandering energy to find a home and settle. Any excess energy that might not have a home is guided back to the lower abdomen to get stored. Make sure to do this visualization slowly. These should be in a sequence of 9 slow and steady orbits. If you choose to cycle this energy too quickly, you may begin to feel lightheaded and dizzy.

It is recommended that you practice this visualization sequence daily this week. Make sure you use your journal to log any experiences that you feel are worthy to capture.

Check-In

Before moving on, let's check on your physical and energetic Earth Phase Imbalances. This is not an evaluation of how you did during the last month, but rather a pulse check to acknowledge and know for your future work.

For each symptom listed, check the box if the symptom is present now or if you've encountered it within the past two weeks.

Potential Physical Earth Phase Imbalances:

- ○ Muscular and lymphatic dysfunction
- ○ Venous disorders
- ○ Digestive and appetite issues
- ○ Weight management difficulties
- ○ Fluid and secretion management issues
- ○ Tissue swelling and gland issues
- ○ General discomfort and pain
- ○ Reproductive and abdominal dysfunctions
- ○ Blood and vascular health issues
- ○ Eye and oral health issues
- ○ Swelling of internal organs

Score:

Potential Energetic Earth Phase Imbalances:

- ○ Challenges with change and orientation: You find it difficult to adapt to new situations or changes in your environment, often feeling disoriented when your routine is disrupted.

- Excessive caregiving or controlling behavior: You may engage in overly protective or controlling behaviors, often putting the needs of others before your own to an unhealthy extent.
- Indecision and uncertainty: You frequently struggle to make decisions, feeling uncertain even when faced with relatively simple choices.
- Self-identity and autonomy issues: You have difficulties maintaining a strong sense of self and often rely on others for validation or direction.
- Focus and thought organization difficulties: You find it challenging to maintain focus or organize your thoughts effectively, which can interfere with completing tasks.
- Dependency and pleasing behavior: You tend to depend too much on others for emotional support or approval and often act primarily to please others at your own expense.
- Unstable thought and decision-making processes: Your thoughts and decisions may frequently change, lacking consistency and often appear erratic or poorly planned.
- Emotional dependence and exaggerated affection: You exhibit a strong emotional attachment to others, often showing affection to an excessive degree that might not be reciprocated or appropriate.
- Inability to progress or stabilize: You often feel stuck, unable to move forward or find stability in various aspects of your life, from relationships to career.
- Interference in personal affairs: You may intrude into the personal matters of others, offering unsolicited advice or assistance, and overstepping boundaries.
- Low energy and depressive states: You frequently experience periods of low energy and feelings of sadness or hopelessness that affect your daily functioning.
- Invasion of personal space and boundaries: You might struggle with respecting the personal space and boundaries of others, often invading their physical or emotional space unintentionally.

○ Excessive worrying and conformity: You tend to worry excessively about various aspects of life and may conform to others' expectations or societal norms without true alignment with your own desires or beliefs.

Score:

The Metal Phase
Fall Season

Metal condenses like air into water,

falling softly, inviting reflection.

It sharpens our vision,

cutting through excess to reveal clarity.

Metal shapes growth,

offering structure and balance to dreams taking form.

The Metal Phase from a Classical Oriental Medicine perspective is linked energetically to the organs of the Lungs and Large Intestine. If we think about this from a broader concept it paints this as the season around breath and release. In fact, the Lungs energetically are responsible for generating our foundational energy as well as serving as a canopy of protection for the other organs.

What we find naturally occurs in this season is a call to reflect and evaluate where we are in life. We make decisions of what to let go of and what we choose to allow to linger. The lingering often occurs as we sit in a state of sadness or grief, over disappointment and betrayal that we've experienced.

The important thing to note about this phase is the innate need to keep this energy moving. It is when it stagnates that it becomes a problem. Often situations that provoked a deep level of sadness or grief, if left untouched, will become magnets seeking out similar vibrational energy that only magnifies the unprocessed emotion.

In this season, you'll be prompted with an active action on odd-numbered weeks where we will invite movement into the Lungs. Then you'll be given the space for evaluation and reflection on the even-numbered weeks. But before we get started, let's first take a pulse check on what active Metal Phase Imbalances you may be experiencing.

Check-In

For each symptom listed, check the box if the symptom is present now or if you've encountered it within the past two weeks.

Potential Physical Metal Phase Imbalances:

- ○ Respiratory issues
- ○ Skin and integumentary issues
- ○ Fluid balance and hydration issues
- ○ Elimination system dysfunctions
- ○ Circulatory system problems
- ○ Nasal and sinus conditions
- ○ Sweat-related symptoms
- ○ Musculoskeletal rigidity
- ○ Emotional trigger-related symptoms
- ○ Cardiorespiratory reflections

Score:

Potential Energetic Metal Phase Imbalances:

- ○ Control and authority issues: You often struggle with situations where you need to assert control or respond to authority, which may result in conflict or discomfort.
- ○ Difficulty with emotional challenges: You find it hard to manage and respond effectively to emotional stress, often feeling overwhelmed or unable to cope.
- ○ Relationship and intimacy difficulties: You experience challenges in forming or maintaining close relationships, often due to fear of intimacy or inability to connect on a deeper level.
- ○ Rigidity in perspectives and behavior: You tend to have a fixed way of thinking and acting, finding it difficult to adapt or consider alternative viewpoints or approaches.
- ○ Need for order and perfection: You have a strong desire for everything to be in order and perfect, which can lead to frustration when things do not meet your high standards.
- ○ Formal and prescribed behaviors: You often adhere strictly to formal rules or socially prescribed behaviors, sometimes at the expense of spontaneity or personal expression.
- ○ Superficial concerns and behaviors: You may focus on surface-level issues or engage in behaviors that lack depth and genuine engagement.
- ○ Discrepancies in beliefs and actions: There is often a gap between what you believe and how you act, which can lead to internal conflict or perceptions of hypocrisy.
- ○ Emotional responsiveness issues: You may have difficulties in responding appropriately to emotional cues or situations, often appearing detached or overly emotional.
- ○ Behavioral standards and conduct: You hold yourself and others to very high standards of behavior, which can lead to judgment or dissatisfaction with people's conduct.

- ○ Elusiveness in convictions: You might show a tendency to be vague or non-committal in your beliefs and opinions, often avoiding taking a firm stance on issues.

Score:

Remember, any of the imbalances you checked are simply your body's way of communicating with you that something is out of alignment. The exercises for this phase will help to restore alignment by releasing what might be causing your energy to stagnate as well as providing nourishment in areas where you've possibly depleted your energetic reserves.

Now you're ready to begin with your first exercise. The way you approach the next pages is completely up to you. However, the chart below will give you a recommendation based off your burnout level score.

- **Stages 1-2**: Follow the structured plan in the book, introducing one new exercise per week.
- **Stages 3-4**: Move to a new exercise only if you have the capacity. Otherwise, repeat the prior exercise or take a pause to rest.
- **Stage 5**: Focus only on the first exercise of the phase. Reflect deeply and discuss your experience with a mental health practitioner.

September

Week 1

For your first week in this season, we are going to focus on breaking up physical stagnation in the Lungs by inviting movement into that meridian. The Lung Meridian starts in the hands and then runs up the arms down the center of the chest into the Lungs.

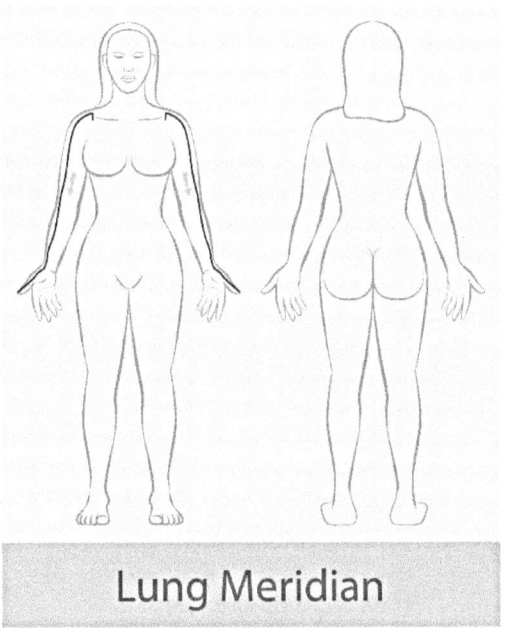

To stimulate movement, we are going to use a technique called Knocking or Tapping. This simply requires you to tap or knock on parts of the body. For this week's exercise, I want you to focus on three specific areas.

1. Begin tapping or knocking on the area shown below, this is an acupuncture point known as Lung 1. Oftentimes I will knock on this point by swinging my fists up to the chest like a gorilla.

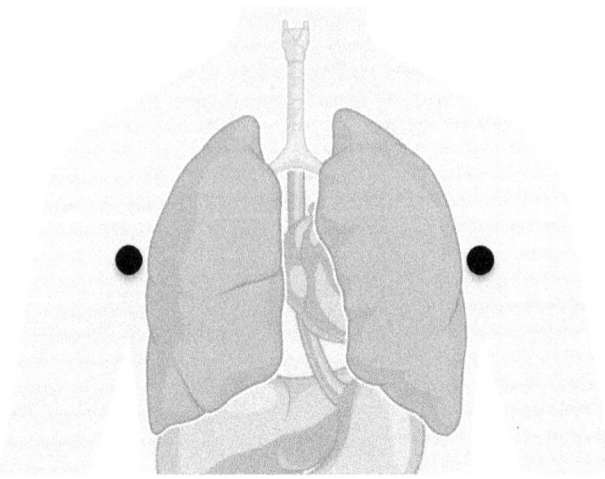

2. Tap and knock Lung 1 on the other side of the body.
3. Lightly tap on your sternum, which is located at the center and front of your chest. Tap or knock lightly up and down.

After you've tapped or knocked on these three areas for about 30-60 seconds each, take a moment to check in with the body and see what you notice. Especially note if any of the areas were tender when you were tapping or knocking.

To fully stimulate the Lungs, please try to do these exercises daily. It should take less than 5 minutes.

Week 2

Now that you've spent a week focusing on moving the energy within the Lungs, you are going to spend this week beginning to check in on what emotional stagnations may be present in this area.

I've already shared that the Lungs energetically are known to be the storage place for stagnated emotions of sadness. But what is the true definition of sadness and how does it impact your energy?

Throughout the even-numbered weeks of this month, we will unpack some Classical Oriental Theory that dives into the energetic dynamics of Sadness.

The following is an excerpt from *The Seven Emotions* by Claude Larre and Elisabeth Rochat De La Vallee:

"Sadness is a rupture with reality in the depths of your being, it is a break-up in yourself between the perception and the acceptance of reality. There is a kind of split. This is the way sadness exhausts vitality."

Get your journal and free-write on the prompts below. Write for no longer than 4 minutes per prompt and make sure you at least linger for 1 minute at each one. Please use a timer, as these are not just recommended time frames. This ensures you will give each one a fair shake while also not falling into the unproductive pit of venting.

Reflective Prompts:

1. What ruptures with reality come to mind?
2. What break-up within yourself have you experienced?
3. Has sadness exhausted you? If so, why do you allow it to linger?

Week 3

This week you'll begin releasing the stagnating emotional energy through breathwork. Please try and complete the exercise below daily.

If you'd prefer to practice this exercise through a guided audio, I've created one for you. You can access it at: **www.HRartInstitute.com**.

1. Begin by focusing on your natural breath, tuning in to your natural rhythm of the inhale and exhale.
2. Continue with your natural breathing rhythm, but guide your inhale down to the belly. When you exhale, empty the belly. Continue this pattern until it is comfortable. It is not necessary to attempt to deepen or elongate the breathing rhythm. You may do so if this happens naturally as the body relaxes, otherwise, stay with the rhythm that is comfortable for you. At no time, should you feel like you are without an adequate amount of breath.
3. Begin incorporating a visual with your inhale. Imagine that the breath is now a white mist that you inhale into your body. Send this white mist into your lungs and large intestine.

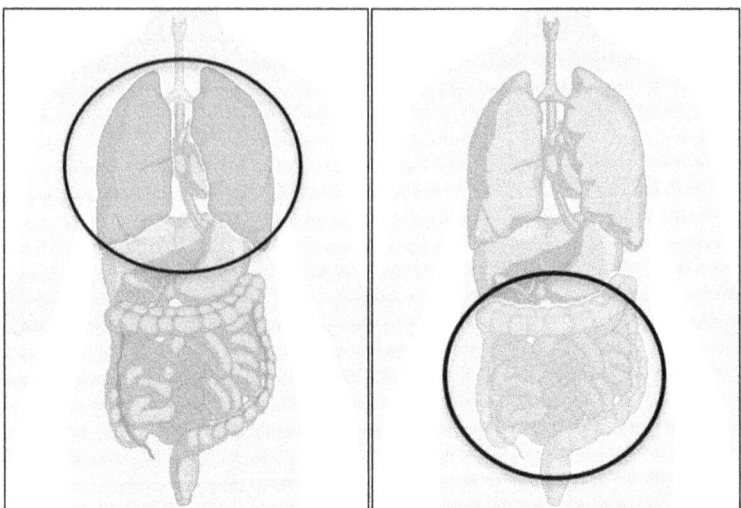

4. Now start exhaling out through the mouth while hearing in your mind or audibly making a *Shhhhh* sound. Imagine this sound vibrating the lungs and large intestine, releasing stagnated emotional and mental energies. See these energies being carried out of the body by the breath on the exhale.

5. Complete 8 repetitions of inhaling the color and exhaling the sound audibly or inaudibly.

6. Next, start exhaling out through the mouth while hearing in your mind or audibly making a *Ssssss* sound. Imagine this sound vibrating the lungs and large intestine, releasing stagnated emotional and mental energies. See these energies being carried out of the body by the breath on the exhale.

7. Complete 8 repetitions of inhaling the color and exhaling the sound audibly or inaudibly.

Week 4

The following is an excerpt from *The Seven Emotions* by Claude Larre and Elisabeth Rochat De La Vallee.

> "In this state of sadness and affliction one is moved at the center. This sadness goes right to the center of the vitality, which could be the Heart or movement of the spirit through the five elements. The sadness just attacks and injures the very inner most part of

life, and there is an interruption of the flowing vitality. Life is lost."

Get your journal and free-write on the prompts below. Remember to write for no longer than 4 minutes per prompt and make sure you at least linger at each for 1 minute.

Reflective Prompts:

1. What sadness is present that hurts your Heart?
2. What interruptions in energy have you experienced that might be linked to stagnant sadness?
3. Have you felt that life has been lost as a result of stagnant sadness?

October

Week 1

From a spiritual energetic perspective, the Metal Phase is known to house the Seven Corporeal Souls, otherwise known as the Po. The Po have similar meaning to the survival mode of human nature sometimes called the Reptilian Brain. They are known for Self-Protection and Self-Preservation. They are the driving force behind your passions, desires, and ambitions in life.

When we are experiencing many energetic blocks or stagnations in this area, we often find that the Po are functioning in a place without healthy boundaries. Where they become ruthless in their need to protect and preserve you, this often translates into encouragement for unhealthy coping strategies to disassociate with how you feel as well as limited perspective in decision making. The Po will aim to guide you toward safety through comfort.

You've just experienced a month of stimulating this energy, moving it, releasing it, and reflecting on it. This week, I invite you to continue doing any of the exercises from last month that have proven beneficial. However, your task for this week is to observe what you naturally move to in this season.

How are your Po protecting you and preserving you? Are these strategies aligned with the path you hope to move forward on? What are they specifically and when did they originate? Is there a connection to the emotion of sadness?

Week 2

Here is the final excerpt from *The Seven Emotions* by Claude Larre and Elisabeth Rochat De La Vallee that you'll explore this season.

"This sadness if often in a dual relationship with profound joy. Profound joy is an open presence, enabling me to accept everything that is in myself, my surroundings, my life. Sadness is the refusal to do this, it is the opposition of that. When one is prey to sadness and affliction, one is without vitality, being without vitality one can no longer ensure the norm."

Get your journal and free-write on the prompts below. Remember to write for no longer 4 minutes per prompt and make sure you at least linger at each for 1 minute.

Reflective Prompts:

- When have you experienced profound joy and acceptance of self?
- How does it feel to think of the concept of holding onto sadness as meaning you are refusing to experience profound joy?
- What is the norm that you no longer experience that you crave?

Week 3

In the beginning of this season, I mentioned how the Metal Phase is responsible for establishing our foundational energy, and that it cultivates this energy from two primary sources:

1. Breath: The air we inhale and exhale
2. Food: The nourishment and nutrients contained within what we eat

This week, your task is to observe your breath and food, specifically, getting curious around how you feel when you breathe and how you feel when you eat.

- Do you find yourself out of breath easily after short walks or climbing stairs?
- Does it feel like you never have enough air?
- Is your breath what easily centers you, so you find yourself relying on deep breaths throughout your day?
- Do you eat? When do you eat?
- How do you feel while eating what you're eating?

- How do you feel before and after you eat?

Knowing that these two life substances are providing for you on an energetic level, use this week to take stock of where you are at.

Week 4

I recognize that this season might have been hard. The passages on sadness that were presented to you for reflection were intentionally selected for their depth. Fall signifies a true transition toward the end of the year. Nature is transforming during this time and so are you. We often say things like we're sad to see the end of summer, however I hope you now recognize that Fall as a season asks you to grieve. Not only to grieve, but to then let go and move on. Within sadness are some of the most powerful lessons of life. It is often here that you find exactly what you need to live with high integrity. Boundaries are ultimately the outcomes.

As this season comes to a close, I want to invite you to reflect on boundaries that need to be established. Personally, I hate the term *boundaries*. I actually started to refer to them as Non-Negotiables. It sounds cold, but after witnessing the true impact that sadness takes on your vitality, you cannot afford to merely experience it on repeat. Non-Negotiables allow you to move forward, in a more aligned way with who you are authentically.

This week, get your journal and simply write. What will you no longer tolerate? What will you let go of? Don't get caught up in the structure or requirements of what should be included. Let it flow, and let the energy move.

Check-In

Before moving on, let's take a minute to check on your physical and energetic Metal Phase Imbalances. This is not an evaluation of how you did during these last two months, but rather a pulse check to acknowledge and know for your future work.

For each symptom listed, check the box if the symptom is present now or if you've encountered it within the past two weeks.

Potential Physical Metal Phase Imbalances:

- ○ Respiratory issues
- ○ Skin and integumentary issues
- ○ Fluid balance and hydration issues
- ○ Elimination system dysfunctions
- ○ Circulatory system problems
- ○ Nasal and sinus conditions
- ○ Sweat-related symptoms
- ○ Musculoskeletal rigidity
- ○ Emotional trigger-related symptoms
- ○ Cardiorespiratory reflections

Score:

Potential Energetic Metal Phase Imbalances:

- ○ Control and authority issues: You often struggle with situations where you need to assert control or respond to authority, which may result in conflict or discomfort.

- ○ Difficulty with emotional challenges: You find it hard to manage and respond effectively to emotional stress, often feeling overwhelmed or unable to cope.
- ○ Relationship and intimacy difficulties: You experience challenges in forming or maintaining close relationships, often due to fear of intimacy or inability to connect on a deeper level.
- ○ Rigidity in perspectives and behavior: You tend to have a fixed way of thinking and acting, finding it difficult to adapt or consider alternative viewpoints or approaches.
- ○ Need for order and perfection: You have a strong desire for everything to be in order and perfect, which can lead to frustration when things do not meet your high standards.
- ○ Formal and prescribed behaviors: You often adhere strictly to formal rules or socially prescribed behaviors, sometimes at the expense of spontaneity or personal expression.
- ○ Superficial concerns and behaviors: You may focus on surface-level issues or engage in behaviors that lack depth and genuine engagement.
- ○ Discrepancies in beliefs and actions: There is often a gap between what you believe and how you act, which can lead to internal conflict or perceptions of hypocrisy.
- ○ Emotional responsiveness issues: You may have difficulties in responding appropriately to emotional cues or situations, often appearing detached or overly emotional.
- ○ Behavioral standards and conduct: You hold yourself and others to very high standards of behavior, which can lead to judgment or dissatisfaction with people's conduct.
- ○ Elusiveness in convictions: You might show a tendency to be vague or non-committal in your beliefs and opinions, often avoiding taking a firm stance on issues.

Score:

The Earth Phase
Supporting Metal into Water

Earth grounds the mind,

a steady foundation for logic to process what we've lived.

Here, reflection deepens,

as we trust ourselves to uncover the true meaning

hidden within life's lessons.

In China, the "Yellow Court" was a term used to refer to the place within the Emperor's Palace where the Ministers (or advisors) would gather to try to understand the will of the Heavens to properly run the affairs of the kingdom. From a Classical Oriental Teaching, within you there is a spiritual energetic center that is called this same term. It functions in a similar fashion, with the Heart as the Emperor and your entire being as the Kingdom. The advisors within you materialize from the spiritual energetic function of the four other major Yin organs, that also happen to correspond to the seasons and the elemental phases.

The energy of the Metal Phase, during this past Fall season, invited you to take stock and evaluate your year and even your lifetime to this point. This energy is designed to support you as you enter this final season that will demand a deeper level of reflection. It will be in Winter when you truly begin to unpack the wisdom you've gained in the last year, that will then prepare you for new growth in the Spring.

Therefore, we will use this seasonal transitional time that is supported by the Earth energy to settle the Metal energy and prepare to welcome the Water energy. Each week during this month, you'll be invited to reflect and release, allowing yourself to start a deeper reflection while also letting go of what will not serve you in the next season.

As you can imagine, the Yellow Court holds many ideas, experiences, and thought patterns that are presented for consideration while determining your future. Not all of these ideas, experiences, or thought patterns are aligned with who you are and therefore are not worthy of necessary consideration. Many times, these ideas or thought patterns were simply projected onto you by others who were not ready to do their own reflection and releasing work. Before you get started, let's first take a pulse check on what active Earth Phase Imbalances you may be experiencing.

Check-In

For each symptom listed, check the box if the symptom is present now or if you've encountered it within the past two weeks.

Potential Physical Earth Phase Imbalances:

- ○ Muscular and lymphatic dysfunction
- ○ Venous disorders
- ○ Digestive and appetite issues
- ○ Weight management difficulties
- ○ Fluid and secretion management issues
- ○ Tissue swelling and gland issues
- ○ General discomfort and pain
- ○ Reproductive and abdominal dysfunctions
- ○ Blood and vascular health issues
- ○ Eye and oral health issues
- ○ Swelling of internal organs

Score:

Potential Energetic Earth Phase Imbalances:

- ○ Challenges with change and orientation: You find it difficult to adapt to new situations or changes in your environment, often feeling disoriented when your routine is disrupted.
- ○ Excessive caregiving or controlling behavior: You may engage in overly protective or controlling behaviors, often putting the needs of others before your own to an unhealthy extent.

- ○ Indecision and uncertainty: You frequently struggle to make decisions, feeling uncertain even when faced with relatively simple choices.
- ○ Self-identity and autonomy issues: You have difficulties maintaining a strong sense of self and often rely on others for validation or direction.
- ○ Focus and thought organization difficulties: You find it challenging to maintain focus or organize your thoughts effectively, which can interfere with completing tasks.
- ○ Dependency and pleasing behavior: You tend to depend too much on others for emotional support or approval and often act primarily to please others at your own expense.
- ○ Unstable thought and decision-making processes: Your thoughts and decisions may frequently change, lacking consistency and often appear erratic or poorly planned.
- ○ Emotional dependence and exaggerated affection: You exhibit a strong emotional attachment to others, often showing affection to an excessive degree that might not be reciprocated or appropriate.
- ○ Inability to progress or stabilize: You often feel stuck, unable to move forward or find stability in various aspects of your life, from relationships to career.
- ○ Interference in personal affairs: You may intrude into the personal matters of others, offering unsolicited advice or assistance, and overstepping boundaries.
- ○ Low energy and depressive states: You frequently experience periods of low energy and feelings of sadness or hopelessness that affect your daily functioning.
- ○ Invasion of personal space and boundaries: You might struggle with respecting the personal space and boundaries of others, often invading their physical or emotional space unintentionally.
- ○ Excessive worrying and conformity: You tend to worry excessively about various aspects of life and may conform to others'

expectations or societal norms without true alignment with your own desires or beliefs.

Score:

_____

Remember, any of the imbalances you checked are simply your body's way of communicating with you that something is out of alignment. The exercises for this phase will help to restore alignment by releasing what might be causing your energy to stagnate as well as providing nourishment in areas where you've possibly depleted your energetic reserves.

Now you're ready to begin with your first exercise. The way you approach the next pages is completely up to you. However, the chart below will give you a recommendation based off your burnout level score.

- **Stages 1-2**: Follow the structured plan in the book, introducing one new exercise per week.
- **Stages 3-4**: Move to a new exercise only if you have the capacity. Otherwise, repeat the prior exercise or take a pause to rest.
- **Stage 5**: Focus only on the first exercise of the phase. Reflect deeply and discuss your experience with a mental health practitioner.

November

Week 1

This week, we will begin by nurturing and overflowing the Yellow Court with healing energy. This energy is easy to tap into at any time because it is the vibrational frequency of gratitude. So, each day to prepare for your practice, please get your journal and write about what you are grateful for. Pour onto the page until you can feel the emotion of gratitude come alive in your body. Keep writing until you have a strong knowing of the vibrational frequency attached to this emotion. Then you can conclude your journal entry and move into the breathwork practice below.

When writing about gratitude in your journal, the more specific and detailed you can be, the more likely you are to generate a stronger vibration within. These specifics can be around something quite small, as there is power in being grateful for each breath or even the warmth of sunlight on your skin.

If you prefer to do this week's exercise following a guided audio, you can access the one I've created for you at: **www.HRartInstitute.com**.

Exercise: Overflowing the Yellow Court with Gratitude

1. Find a comfortable seat and take a moment to ground yourself. Feel connected to the ground beneath you, either through your feet or your spine.

2. Now begin turning inward by following the natural rhythm of your breath. Notice all the subtle details of the inhale and all the subtle details of the exhale.

3. Recognize that your inhale is innately inviting new nourishment into your body, while your exhale is releasing out of your body anything that no longer serves you.

4. Focus your attention on your Yellow Court, located right in the center of your digestive organs, below the rib cage.

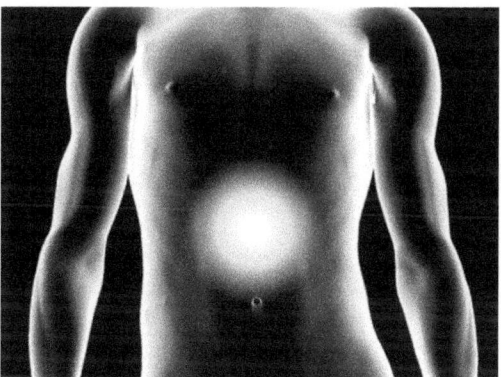

5. On your next inhale, imagine your breath is a Golden Yellow. As it enters the body, it is intuitively guided to the Yellow Court, filling the area. Continue this pattern until you are comfortable breathing in the Golden Yellow.

6. Now begin to focus on the vibrational frequency of gratitude that you identified while preparing for this practice. Allow this frequency to infuse with the Golden Yellow on each breath. Feel it being carried to the Yellow Court and filling that area.

7. Continue this breathwork sequence until you feel your Yellow Court overflowing with Golden Yellow Light and gratitude.

It is recommended that you practice this exercise daily this week. Make sure you use your journal to log any experiences that you feel are worthy to capture.

Week 2

This week we are going to do an exercise that is focused on releasing what is not yours. Specifically, this week we will focus on emotion. It is likely the things that are needed to be released during this exercise are causing unnecessary worry. You may be worrying or obsessing over a particular individual or situation, believing that it shares some insight into who you are, how you failed, or what you need to do differently. To be honest, usually the only wisdom these situations of worry have to share with you, are times when people have violated your boundaries. This should signal to you that they are not worth worrying about.

If you prefer to do this week's exercise following a guided audio, you can access the one I've created for you at: **www.HRartInstitute.com**.

Exercise: Not Mine to Worry About Vortex

1. Find a comfortable position either standing, sitting, or even laying down.
2. Begin turning inward by following the natural rhythm of your breath. Notice all the subtle details of the inhale and all the subtle details of the exhale.
3. Now imagine a cylinder of energy emerging from the Earth that rises up and encompasses your entire body.
4. Imagine the cylinder of energy starting to rotate slowly counterclockwise. As it rotates, you can feel it beginning to collect and pull things from your energetic body.
5. Tune in and set the intention, *"Take what is not mine to worry about."*
6. Allow the cylinder to continue spinning and collecting, noticing that it is slowly becoming a vortex that funnels the turbid energetic debris back into the Earth for recycling.
7. When you feel the vortex is finished collecting, or you feel as if you are finished releasing for this practice, allow the vortex to slow down in movement. When it comes to stillness, slowly allow the energy to sink back into the earth and begin to wake up your body.

It is recommended that you practice this exercise daily this week. Make sure you use your journal to log any experiences that you feel are worthy to capture.

Week 3

This week's exercise is designed with the intention to vibrate and release stagnation in the Yellow Court. It will be similar to the exercise you practiced in Week 1 but will incorporate sound to facilitate a gentle vibration to encourage further release.

I highly recommend that you complete this exercise daily. After your practice, make sure to journal and log anything that surfaced or things that you experienced. If you'd prefer to practice this exercise through a guided audio, you can access it at: **www.HRartInstitute.com**.

1. Begin by focusing on your natural breath, tuning into your natural rhythm of the inhale and exhale.

2. Begin incorporating a visual with your inhale. Imagine that the breath is now a golden yellow mist that you inhale into your body. Send this golden yellow mist and overflow your Yellow Court.

3. Now start exhaling out through the mouth while hearing in your mind or audibly making a *Whooo* sound. Imagine this sound vibrating the Yellow Court, releasing stagnated emotional and mental energies. See these energies being carried out of the body by the breath on the exhale.

4. Complete at least 8 repetitions of inhaling the color and exhaling the sound audibly or inaudibly. Feel free to continue the practice longer, if you feel called.

Week 4

Our final exercise for this month will be exactly like the one we practiced in week 2, with a slight change in the intention. The focus of this vortex will be to release what is not yours to think about. Specifically, these are thoughts that are causing you to doubt yourself. During the exercise, allow yourself to trust that you know at a deeper level what you need to hold onto. Therefore, those thoughts and even situations or people that you feel compelled to let go, let them go. They are not worthy of being a source of doubt. They are not worthy to influence or impact how you see yourself. If you prefer to do this week's exercise following a guided audio, you can access the one I've created for you at: **www.HRartInstitute.com**.

Exercise: The Doubt Free Vortex

1. Find a comfortable position either standing, sitting, or even laying down.

2. Begin turning inward by following the natural rhythm of your breath. Notice all the subtle details of the inhale and all the subtle details of the exhale.

3. Now imagine a cylinder of energy emerging from the Earth that rises up and encompasses your entire body.

4. Imagine the cylinder of energy starting to rotate slowly counterclockwise. As it rotates, you can feel it beginning to collect and pull things from your energetic body.

5. Tune in and set the intention, *"Take what is not mine to think about."*

6. Allow the cylinder to continue spinning and collecting, noticing that it is slowly becoming a vortex that funnels the turbid energetic debris back into the Earth for recycling.

7. When you feel the vortex is finished collecting, or you feel as if you are finished releasing for this practice, allow the vortex to slow down in movement.

8. When it comes to stillness, allow yourself to sit in the cylinder of Earth energy, and imagine filling it with a beautiful navy blue color.

9. Breathe into this space while saying, "I no longer doubt myself. I trust me." Sit in this space for 1-3 minutes.

10. Allow the cylinder to dissipate and slowly bring your attention back to the room that you're in.

It is recommended that you practice this exercise daily this week. Make sure you use your journal to log any experiences that you feel are worthy to capture.

Check-In

Before moving on, let's take a minute to check on your physical and energetic Earth Phase Imbalances. This is not an evaluation of how you did during the last month, but rather a pulse check to acknowledge and know for your future work.

For each symptom listed, check the box if the symptom is present now or if you've encountered it within the past two weeks.

Potential Physical Earth Phase Imbalances:

- ○ Muscular and lymphatic dysfunction
- ○ Venous disorders
- ○ Digestive and appetite issues
- ○ Weight management difficulties
- ○ Fluid and secretion management issues
- ○ Tissue swelling and gland issues
- ○ General discomfort and pain
- ○ Reproductive and abdominal dysfunctions
- ○ Blood and vascular health issues
- ○ Eye and oral health issues
- ○ Swelling of internal organs

Score:

Potential Energetic Earth Phase Imbalances:

- ○ Challenges with change and orientation: You find it difficult to adapt to new situations or changes in your environment, often feeling disoriented when your routine is disrupted.

- ○ Excessive caregiving or controlling behavior: You may engage in overly protective or controlling behaviors, often putting the needs of others before your own to an unhealthy extent.
- ○ Indecision and uncertainty: You frequently struggle to make decisions, feeling uncertain even when faced with relatively simple choices.
- ○ Self-identity and autonomy issues: You have difficulties maintaining a strong sense of self and often rely on others for validation or direction.
- ○ Focus and thought organization difficulties: You find it challenging to maintain focus or organize your thoughts effectively, which can interfere with completing tasks.
- ○ Dependency and pleasing behavior: You tend to depend too much on others for emotional support or approval and often act primarily to please others at your own expense.
- ○ Unstable thought and decision-making processes: Your thoughts and decisions may frequently change, lacking consistency and often appear erratic or poorly planned.
- ○ Emotional dependence and exaggerated affection: You exhibit a strong emotional attachment to others, often showing affection to an excessive degree that might not be reciprocated or appropriate.
- ○ Inability to progress or stabilize: You often feel stuck, unable to move forward or find stability in various aspects of your life, from relationships to career.
- ○ Interference in personal affairs: You may intrude into the personal matters of others, offering unsolicited advice or assistance, and overstepping boundaries.
- ○ Low energy and depressive states: You frequently experience periods of low energy and feelings of sadness or hopelessness that affect your daily functioning.
- ○ Invasion of personal space and boundaries: You might struggle with respecting the personal space and boundaries of others, often invading their physical or emotional space unintentionally.

○ Excessive worrying and conformity: You tend to worry excessively about various aspects of life and may conform to others' expectations or societal norms without true alignment with your own desires or beliefs.

Score:

PAUSE
IS NOT
FAILURE.

IT'S WISDOM

IN ACTION

The Water Phase
Winter Season

Water nourishes and clears the way,

sustaining growth through deep reflection.

It washes away obstructions,

extinguishing fire when its burn becomes too much.

In the quiet of ash,

water invites rest and renewal.

The Water Phase in Classical Oriental Theory is linked to the organs of the Kidneys and Bladder. The Kidneys play an important role energetically as they are known to hold your prenatal and postnatal essence. In other words, the Kidneys serve as your energetic reserves, consisting of what energy you brought into this life and all that you have acquired throughout your life. It is this concept that helps to explain why, as a child, you may have been like me, described as an "Energizer Bunny" who would run laps in between bites during meals. Or perhaps as a child you preferred less active play, things that required less energy, or maybe you were even an excellent frequent napper. It is a myth to believe that all children come into this world with boundless energy. We all come into this life with a unique level of energy.

We also each tend to our energy differently throughout life. We cultivate energy through our choices—from what we choose to eat to how we choose to spend our days. Classical Oriental Theory, particularly around the Water Phase, speaks to the ability to care for your vitality and longevity and even increase it, meaning that the idea of a predetermined amount of energy tied to your lifespan is a myth as well.

Now this phase does not strictly cater to the energetic essence and reserves from a physical living standpoint, but also from a spiritual aspect. This means that the Water Phase is home to your Will Power. It is this energetic powerhouse that enables you to move forward stepping into your power and making things happen. The desires of the Heart, your dreams, are only able to materialize when this Phase is balanced.

This season is also the most Yin time of year, and therefore, during this time, you'll be prompted every week to either turn inward or engage in reflection. As you participate in these activities, know that at times you can feel as though your thought patterns are taking a dark turn. Yin in its organic nature is still, dark, and cold. This does not mean evil, bad, or ugly. These are things that our culture has instilled within us. Instead, view this discomfort as a new level of depth. It is in these depths that we have the opportunity to truly heal, grow, and evolve to a higher vibration. Before you get started, let's first take a pulse check on what active Water Phase Imbalances you may be experiencing.

Check-In

For each symptom listed, check the box if the symptom is present now or if you've encountered it within the past two weeks.

Potential Physical Water Phase Imbalances:

- Memory problems and trouble focusing
- Difficulties with movement and sensing changes
- Alterations in bone, joint, and dental health
- Issues with physical development and reproductive health
- Problems with managing body fluids
- Cysts, swelling, or hardening in reproductive and urinary organs
- Irregular sleep patterns, including trouble waking up
- Vision and hearing problems
- Ringing in the ears (tinnitus)
- Weakness and stiffness in the body and joints
- Wear and tear on spinal disks and cartilage
- Cold feelings in the lower body
- Need to urinate more often
- Bone thinning (osteoporosis)
- Early signs of aging (gray hair, hair loss, wrinkles)
- Fertility issues or sexual health problems
- Fatigue or low energy levels
- Reduced appetite
- Weakness in abdominal muscles
- Changes in skin color or texture
- Headaches, especially around the eyes or top of the head
- Decreased sweating and less frequent urination
- Stiffening of blood vessels and cartilage
- Kidney or bladder stones
- Development of bony growths
- Digestive issues
- Receding gums (gum health problems)
- Sleeping less than usual

- ○ Constipation or trouble with bowel movements
- ○ High blood pressure (hypertension)

Score:

Potential Energetic Water Phase Imbalances:

- ○ Social interaction challenges: You may find it difficult to engage in social activities or feel uncomfortable during social interactions.
- ○ Communication difficulties: You might struggle to clearly express your thoughts and feelings to others.
- ○ Discomfort in social exposure: You could feel uneasy or anxious when you are the center of attention or in large groups.
- ○ Critical behavior: You often find yourself criticizing others or focusing on their faults
- ○ Negative worldview: You tend to see the world in a negative light and often expect the worst outcomes.
- ○ Health anxiety: You frequently worry about your health and may be preoccupied with fears of becoming ill.
- ○ Immobility episodes: There are times when you feel so overwhelmed that you become physically immobile or emotionally unresponsive.
- ○ Observational preference: You prefer to watch others rather than participate in activities directly.
- ○ Imaginative thought processes: Your thinking often involves fantasy or unrealistic scenarios.
- ○ Financial frugality: You are extremely cautious about spending money, often to the point of avoiding necessary expenses.
- ○ Distracted by thoughts: You frequently find your mind wandering, and you have trouble focusing on the task at hand.
- ○ Intense observation: You tend to observe people and situations very closely, often noticing details that others miss.

- ○ Aloofness: You generally keep your distance from others and might come off as detached or uninterested.
- ○ Behavioral analysis: You often analyze people's behavior, trying to understand their motives and actions.
- ○ Unconventional behavior: Your behavior or thinking often deviates from the norm, and you are not afraid to be different.
- ○ Suspicion and covetousness: You may be overly suspicious of others' motives or envious of their achievements and possessions.

Score:

Remember, any of the imbalances you checked are simply your body's way of communicating with you that something is out of alignment. The exercises for this phase will help to restore alignment by releasing what might be causing your energy to stagnate as well as providing nourishment in areas where you've possibly depleted your energetic reserves.

Now you're ready to begin with your first exercise. The way you approach the next pages is completely up to you. However, the chart below will give you a recommendation based off your burnout level score.

- **Stages 1-2**: Follow the structured plan in the book, introducing one new exercise per week.
- **Stages 3-4**: Move to a new exercise only if you have the capacity. Otherwise, repeat the prior exercise or take a pause to rest.
- **Stage 5**: Focus only on the first exercise of the phase. Reflect deeply and discuss your experience with a mental health practitioner.

December

Week 1

For your first week in this season, we are going to begin by playing with stillness. I know this can be uncomfortable sometimes, so we are going to do it with a breathwork pattern that is often used for stress relief. This week will be about prioritizing the breathwork and giving yourself time for stillness. Next week, we will build upon this skillset to go a bit deeper. Before practicing the exercise below, find a place that is quiet with limited distractions and set a timer for 10 minutes

1. Begin focusing on your breath, noticing your natural rhythm of the inhale and exhale. Focus on inhaling and exhaling through the nose and keeping your mouth gently closed. The entire face should feel relaxed while you are breathing.
2. Now imagine that the breath coming into your nose is a deep navy blue mist. As it enters the body, it travels to your kidneys, filling them with this new nourishing energy.
3. Once comfortable with inhaling the color, begin counting your breaths. Inhale for a count of 4, hold the breath for a count of 4, and then exhale for a count of 4. Attempt to make this your natural rhythm, while still continuing to inhale the color.
4. Continue until your timer signals the end of the 10 minutes.

If you find it challenging to carry out the visual of seeing the inhaled color making it to the kidneys, simply focus on the color during the inhale and trust your intention. Know that because you've set the intention to use that energy for the kidneys, your body will guide it there for you while you focus on breath counts.

Attempt to do this practice daily and make sure to journal anything you notice. This could be the literal reaction to the experience of this exercise being hard or boring or relaxing, or it could be a realization that shifts are happening that have no explanation except for this practice. Or maybe you naturally find yourself engaging in this practice throughout the day, perhaps capturing what life event or set of circumstances caused this to happen.

Week 2

Now that you've spent a week beginning to play with breath holding, we are going to expand on it by engaging your intuition. This is going to invite you to let go of the logical structure of the counts that were provided last week to instead listen to your body as it guides you through the sequence.

The most important thing to remember is we never want to put ourselves in a position where we are lacking air. You should not feel like you are exasperated or gasping for breath. If you find yourself falling into this pattern, slow down and find your natural rhythm. Give yourself permission to take a couple of deep inhales to catch your breath.

Breath holding is a practice that is part of Dao Yin Training and many practitioners engage in it with the hopes of what they may see or learn during the holds. It is said that the breath holds can become a gateway to a different level of subconscious wisdom. For our purposes, this translates into a method for a deeper dive within yourself. As you begin the modified practice below, pay particular attention to what presents itself during your breath holds (i.e. colors, random thoughts, or even phrases). We will still stick to the 10-minute time frame, however, please feel free to extend your stillness sessions if you want to.

1. Once comfortable inhaling the navy blue color, begin to tune into your inhale. Inhale to a place that is comfortable and then exhale out to a place that is comfortable.
2. Now, play with the edges of the inhale and exhale, to see if you can extend them just a nudge.
3. Begin incorporating a breath hold, but only hold for what's comfortable, then exhale out.

4. After you are comfortable with the innate rhythm of the inhale, hold, and exhale, start to play with the edges of the hold, nudging them just a bit longer.
5. Continue until your timer signals the end of the session.

At the conclusion of your session, capture your experience in your journal. Recognize that you may see nothing during your breath holds and that's okay. Just capture what occurred with no judgment, seeing these entries more like logs to capture future growth or barriers.

Week 3

This week we're going to transition to our reflective work for the season. However, I want you to continue the stillness sessions for the rest of the season, engaging in the breath holding work and capturing your outcomes. If possible, I highly encourage you to aim for 20 minutes a day, ideally in one session, but if needed, it can be split into two 10-minute sessions.

The Water Phase and Kidneys are known for being the foundation for all Yin and Yang energies within the body. In other words, this energy center is the basis for your ability to ultimately find balance. What is interesting is that despite this season being naturally overtly Yin, our culture has filled it with Yang. A time when the active Yang nature of us should be dormant is forced to engage in hectic holiday plans and forced excessive demands for connection.

To gain an understanding of how this dynamic is impacting you personally, we are going to do a bit of a Yin Yang inventory of your life this season.

In your journal, create an entry where you draw a line down the center of the page to make two columns. Label one column Yin and the other Yang. To begin, let's just start with your day. I want you to go through your planned activities for the day in as much detail as possible and place them in either the Yin or Yang column.

The Yang column will be for activities that require you to be active—social gatherings, shopping, errands, work, cleaning, and so on. Typically, these types of activities fulfill a demand from an external source.

The Yin column will be for activities that invite you to turn inward and honor rest and recovery for your body. This will typically be self-care acts, like massage, or your stillness sessions. This could include times during the day when you find yourself in reflection or contemplation of greater meaning for your days and relationships.

I want to be clear that both types of activities require energy. It is simply a different type of energy. Don't assume that Yin activities are lazy activities. Something like watching TV might be a Yang activity if it appeases your social demand for your time. It might be Yin if you find yourself being prompted by what you're watching to examine your own life. It could also be a numbing or coping strategy that is neither truly Yin or Yang, just more like an energy depletion activity because there's not enough left in your energetic reserves to do much of anything else.

Try doing a journal entry for each day this week, then as a bonus, perhaps try a collective look at the entire season, by looking at your monthly calendar and taking stock of what you already have planned for December and January.

The goal is to get a tangible look at the balance between Yin and Yang on a daily basis. You may want to revisit these entries at the end of the day to add any last-minute activities that occurred, errands that came up, or even Yin moments that found their way in.

Week 4

After taking stock last week, you might be thinking that you had pretty good balance, or perhaps you discovered that your daily composition of Yin and Yang is not balanced at all. That activity is one you should examine and evaluate on an ongoing basis, typically looking at your week as a whole, or even your month. The more intentional you are about the balance between Yin and Yang, the more likely you are to live in a more balanced fashion.

That said, there are two seasons that encourage us to immerse ourselves in strictly Yang or strictly Yin. Summer, which is linked to the Fire Phase, invites us to embrace Yang. But Winter begs us to embrace the Yin.

This week I want you to focus on embracing the Yin by identifying some intentional Yin practices—an afternoon nap, doubling up your daily stillness sessions, journaling with reflective practice, meditation class, massages, adult coloring, puzzles. Find activities that serve your Yin side.

It's likely that these activities have already been presenting themselves and perhaps you simply needed the permission to partake in them.

It is important to sit in your Yin side and know what it's like to sit in the quiet. Use your journal to capture whatever comes up, even if it's a bit scary. Trust that what is being presented is being asked to be examined for your highest good.

January

Week 1

January is often filled with personal self-care challenges to use the first of the year as a reset—an opportunity to have a fresh start at pursuing your goals and chasing your dreams. However, the Yin season still has a strong hold on you, and what it asks is for you to continue looking inward.

We often resist this task because if we are lacking energetic reserves and the tank is a bit empty, what bubbles up as the psycho-emotional imbalance is fear—specifically, a fear of the unknown or future. In fact, our extremely wise bodies use fear as the tactic to get us not to move forward exerting more energy. It's a survival tactic with the sole purpose of protecting those dwindling reserves.

This week, instead of answering what you want for this year, I want you to answer what you are afraid of. Get out your journal and let it all out, freely writing about what you are scared of this year.

Week 2

These next two weeks, we are going to introduce some Medical Qigong exercises that are focused on building up your energetic reserves. The first exercise is called the 1-4 Meditation. If you prefer to listen to the guided audio that I've created for you, you can access it at: **www.HRartInstitute.com.**

Before beginning this exercise, check in on your current energy level. On a scale of 1-10, where is your energy now? (1 = super low, 10 = extremely high) Make note of this in your journal.

1-4 Meditation:

1. Prepare for the meditation by sitting in a chair, with your feet flat on the ground beneath you, preferably barefoot. Begin tuning into your natural rhythm of breath, breathing in and out through the nose.

2. Imagine a golden smile floating down from the sun. When it touches the top of your head, you feel its warmth as it begins to travel down the front of your body. It travels over the face, chest, arms, torso, thighs, knees, and feet. Imagine the warmth relaxing any tension or discomfort it finds along the way.

3. Imagine a second golden smile floating down from the sun. When it touches the top of your head, you feel its warmth as it begins to travel down the back of your body. It travels down the back of your head, shoulders, spine, buttons, back of the legs, heels, and bottom of the feet. Imagine the warmth relaxing any tension or discomfort it finds along the way.

4. Imagine a final golden smile floating down from the sun. When it touches the top of your head, you feel its warmth sink into the body, filling the entire body. As it does so, it settles any tension or discomfort it finds on a physical, emotional, and even mental level.

5. Now bring your attention to your feet and imagine them sinking into the earth as if they are becoming one. You can no longer tell where your feet end and the surface beneath you begins.

6. Imagine tree roots emerging from your feet, further connecting you to the earth. They extend deep into the earth's core, running at least two lengths of the height of your body.

7. On your next breath, begin to activate these tree roots, allowing them to absorb the earth's energy. Inhale that energy up the tree roots into your legs and up your spine. Exhale the energy down from the top of the head, down your chest and into your lower abdomen and kidneys. Continue this breathing sequence until you overflow the kidneys and lower abdomen with earth energy.

8. To conclude this meditation, begin focusing on your natural breath again. Allow your tree roots to dissolve and your feet to disconnect

from the surface beneath you. Take your time to bring your attention back to the space you are in.

Afterwards, check in on your energy level and give it a number on a scale of 1-10. Make note in your journal of any changes and anything else that might be important to note about your experiences during the meditation.

If possible, complete this meditation at least four times this week. If you can, add this meditation to your daily stillness sessions for the week.

As you embrace more stillness and these opportunities to go inward, make sure to capture what surfaces while doing this work, never losing sight that this season is about reflection and taking stock at some of the deepest levels. Write it all down, capturing it all in your journal. Nothing is coincidental. Everything serves a purpose. You just might be too in the weeds to see it right now.

Week 3

This week we will continue to use Medical Qigong exercises to build up your energetic reserves. This week's exercises are typically used as a warm-up, to activate or wake up the kidneys. Often Qigong teachers will share with their students that they should practice this exercise when they feel low on energy. It is said that it can be just as good as that afternoon cup of coffee or whatever midday energy booster you may have found.

This exercise utilizes the technique of gently tapping or knocking on the body with your hands. For this practice, we will be focusing our Tapping or Knocking on the lower half of the Bladder and Kidney Meridians that run through the legs.

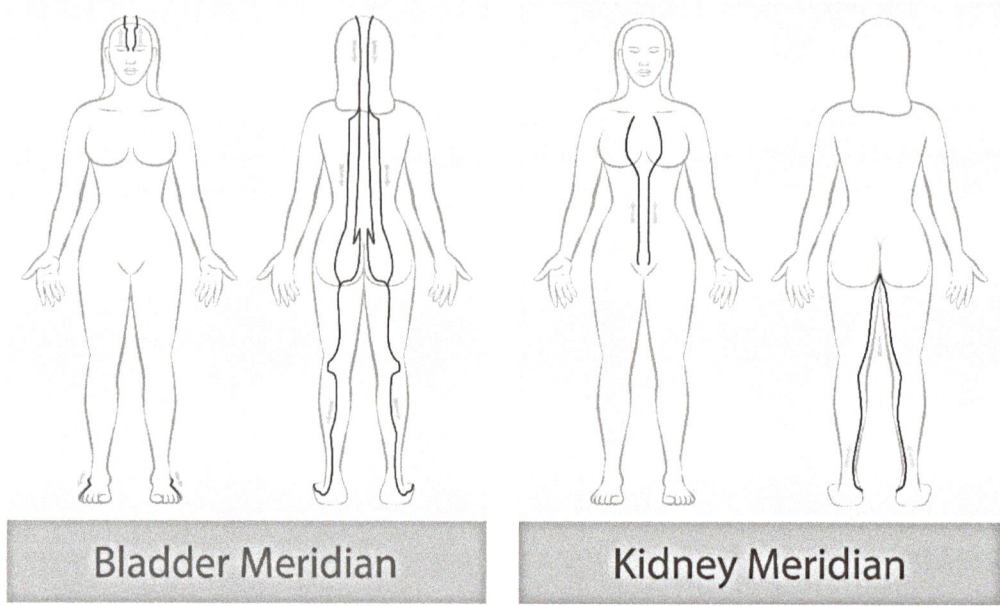

Bladder Meridian   **Kidney Meridian**

When it comes to energy flow and even feeling energy, most people can easily feel energy in the upper portion of their body. It is the lower half where we find ourselves often feeling less movement which could be due to some stagnation. Bringing new energy into the body is only effective if it is able to flow freely and properly circulate.

Before beginning the exercise sequence below, I would like you to check in on your energy levels. Assign it a number on the scale of 1-10, with 1 being super low and 10 being the highest. Write it down in your journal and then make sure to check in after you complete the exercise as well. Remember, this is strictly for increased awareness, so don't get caught up if the number didn't change much or not at all. Part of this process is identifying what works and what doesn't, while also having a log to look back on in case something does turn out to work well over time. Slower progressions might be harder to see at the moment, but will become evident to you at some point.

If you prefer to watch the video that I've created for you rather than following the practice below, you can access it at: **www.HRartInstitute.com**.

Tapping/Knocking for the Kidneys:

1. Begin knocking with your fists lightly at the crevice where your legs connect to your body.

2. Continue knocking but move the movement to the outside of your body, lightly tapping or knocking on your hips.

3. Begin moving your taps and knocks again down the outside of your legs, all the way down to the feet.

4. Then tap and knock up the insides of your legs, until you return to the starting position in Step 1.

5. Continue the sequence of Steps 1-4 for 6-8 rounds.

6. Now bring your focus to the knees. Begin by gently knocking or tapping on the outside of both knees.

7. Then begin to knock or tap on the inside of both knees.

8. Focus on cupping each knee separately, tapping and knocking on the sides but also the top and bottom portion of each knee.

9. Finally, tap or knock on the back of the knees.

The pressure for your tapping and knocking should be firm, but not painful. This exercise should not feel like you are beating yourself up.

Make sure to log your experiences, and if possible, complete this set daily this week.

Ideally, if you could prioritize extending your stillness sessions this week, you could add this as your warm-up before your breath holding work and then end with the 1-4 meditation that we practiced last week.

This season is about embracing Yin, and in these final weeks, my hope is that it becomes natural to surrender to this stillness for longer periods of time.

Week 4

For this final week of the season, I want to give you a chance to play with the true power of the depths of Yin. Earlier this season we talked about the tendency for fear to rise when we experience imbalances in this phase. While fear is often triggered by the imbalance, this is only one aspect of fear that presents itself.

Our culture has taught us that what lives in the dark is scary and not meant to see the light of day. In the Classical Oriental teachings around Yin, which are these dark depths, instead of scary things we should hide from the world, it is in this place that we have the ability to tap into deep wisdom. Even knowing this, the idea of going into this dark deep place can feel overwhelming and often prompts the fear of *what if* I never return.

Personally, I have gone down a rabbit hole that then felt like a dark deep spiral and I struggled to ground again. Grounding is essential, because without it we are unable to make use of this wisdom we tap into. Instead we simply disassociate and leave our body, determining that it is no longer a place where we are safe.

As you continue to heal, this exercise will hopefully instill in you a skillset to tap into this wisdom without fear of losing yourself.

My close friend and mentor taught me this visualization exercise. If you prefer to listen to the guided audio that I've created for you, you can access it at: **www.HRartInstitute.com**.

Buckets of Wisdom Visualization:

1. Close your eyes and begin to tune into your natural breath, embracing your innate rhythm as you inhale and exhale.

2. Imagine that you are sitting on the ledge of a cliff with your legs dangling over the side. Take a moment and feel rooted through your spine. Your spine is connected to the earth, allowing you to feel supported and safe.

3. Your feet feel free and light. Imagine swinging them a bit in a playful fashion. As you look down, all you see is darkness. You have no idea how deep it is below or what might be down there.

4. If you feel nervous or if anxiety begins to rise in your chest, take a few deep inhales and exhale out through the mouth on an inaudible *Haaaa*, releasing that built-up energy. While doing this, tell yourself that the fear has no basis. There is nothing to be afraid of.

5. Once you are settled, beside you appears a bucket with a long piece of strong sturdy rope attached to it.

6. Use your mind to place an imaginary intention in that bucket. This intention should be around some sort of clarity or wisdom that you

seek. Think less about a specific question and more about a particular circumstance or situation.

7. Now gently lower the bucket into the darkness, to whatever depth you feel comfortable. Pause and allow it to sit for a moment, almost like you are fishing. Use this time to be playful again, maybe swinging your feet in the open air and being curious about what lies below.

8. When ready, gently pull the bucket back up to the surface. Energetically investigate the bucket or maybe dip into the bucket and sit with what is presented.

9. If you feel called, you can return the bucket down for a few more rounds, but don't fall into the mode of trying to force clarity or answers. The wisdom should flow freely.

After you finish your visualization exercise, capture everything in your journal, even if it seems pointless. We often have expectations on how wisdom should present itself, when in actuality it communicates to us in the most subtle, gentle ways.

Feel free to play with this visualization exercise in the stillness sessions that you've been embracing. You could tap as a warm-up, practice breath holding, and then do this exercise—or any combination of exercises that we've introduced this season. Find what works and resonates with you. Make sure to capture these sequences down as well in your journal, so you have a personalized road map when you dive back into the Yin next Winter.

Check-In

Before moving on, let's take a minute to check on your physical and energetic Water Phase Imbalances. This is not an evaluation of how you did during these last two months, but rather a pulse check to acknowledge and know for your future work.

For each symptom listed, check the box if the symptom is present now or if you've encountered it within the past two weeks.

Potential Physical Water Phase Imbalances:

- ○ Memory problems and trouble focusing
- ○ Difficulties with movement and sensing changes
- ○ Alterations in bone, joint, and dental health
- ○ Issues with physical development and reproductive health
- ○ Problems with managing body fluids
- ○ Cysts, swelling, or hardening in reproductive and urinary organs
- ○ Irregular sleep patterns, including trouble waking up
- ○ Vision and hearing problems
- ○ Ringing in the ears (tinnitus)
- ○ Weakness and stiffness in the body and joints
- ○ Wear and tear on spinal disks and cartilage
- ○ Cold feelings in the lower body
- ○ Need to urinate more often
- ○ Bone thinning (osteoporosis)
- ○ Early signs of aging (gray hair, hair loss, wrinkles)
- ○ Fertility issues or sexual health problems
- ○ Fatigue or low energy levels
- ○ Reduced appetite

- ○ Weakness in abdominal muscles
- ○ Changes in skin color or texture
- ○ Headaches, especially around the eyes or top of the head
- ○ Decreased sweating and less frequent urination
- ○ Stiffening of blood vessels and cartilage
- ○ Kidney or bladder stones
- ○ Development of bony growths
- ○ Digestive issues
- ○ Receding gums (gum health problems)
- ○ Sleeping less than usual
- ○ Constipation or trouble with bowel movements
- ○ High blood pressure (hypertension)

Score:

Potential Energetic Water Phase Imbalances:

- ○ Social interaction challenges: You may find it difficult to engage in social activities or feel uncomfortable during social interactions.
- ○ Communication difficulties: You might struggle to clearly express your thoughts and feelings to others.
- ○ Discomfort in social exposure: You could feel uneasy or anxious when you are the center of attention or in large groups.
- ○ Critical behavior: You often find yourself criticizing others or focusing on their faults
- ○ Negative worldview: You tend to see the world in a negative light and often expect the worst outcomes.
- ○ Health anxiety: You frequently worry about your health and may be preoccupied with fears of becoming ill.

- ○ Immobility episodes: There are times when you feel so overwhelmed that you become physically immobile or emotionally unresponsive.
- ○ Observational preference: You prefer to watch others rather than participate in activities directly.
- ○ Imaginative thought processes: Your thinking often involves fantasy or unrealistic scenarios.
- ○ Financial frugality: You are extremely cautious about spending money, often to the point of avoiding necessary expenses.
- ○ Distracted by thoughts: You frequently find your mind wandering, and you have trouble focusing on the task at hand.
- ○ Intense observation: You tend to observe people and situations very closely, often noticing details that others miss.
- ○ Aloofness: You generally keep your distance from others and might come off as detached or uninterested.
- ○ Behavioral analysis: You often analyze people's behavior, trying to understand their motives and actions.
- ○ Unconventional behavior: Your behavior or thinking often deviates from the norm, and you are not afraid to be different.
- ○ Suspicion and covetousness: You may be overly suspicious of others' motives or envious of their achievements and possessions.

Score:

The Earth Phase
Supporting Water into Wood

Earth cradles the seeds of reflection,

nurtured by the depths we've explored.

Here, outcomes take root,

ready to be planted and watered with intention.

Through deep connection,

new growth is infused with the strength to thrive.

From a Classical Oriental Theory, there is a spiritual component to the Earth Phase that is connected to the Spleen and Stomach organs. This spiritual component is called the Yi. In some translations, the teachings describe the function of this spirit as the great translator of the Heart. When balanced, it is able to give clear direction to the Kidneys, whose spiritual function is focused on Willpower, about what specific actions to take to begin materializing your Heart's desires.

Specifically in this seasonal transition, the Yi can provide the foundation for vision and planning which come into play when we move fully into

Spring. However, for this transition period between the seasons we will be focusing on the relationship between the Water Phase and the Earth Phase and the impact that a season devoted to Yin may have as you begin to wake to the callings of beginning to move forward with new growth.

During this month, you'll be prompted to practice breathwork on weeks 1 and 3. Then you'll be given the space for reflection in weeks 2 and 4. But before we get started, let's first take a pulse check on what active Earth Phase Imbalances you may be experiencing.

Check-In

For each symptom listed, check the box if the symptom is present now or if you've encountered it within the past two weeks.

Potential Physical Earth Phase Imbalances:

- ○ Muscular and lymphatic dysfunction
- ○ Venous disorders
- ○ Digestive and appetite issues
- ○ Weight management difficulties
- ○ Fluid and secretion management issues
- ○ Tissue swelling and gland issues
- ○ General discomfort and pain
- ○ Reproductive and abdominal dysfunctions
- ○ Blood and vascular health issues
- ○ Eye and oral health issues
- ○ Swelling of internal organs

Score:

Potential Energetic Earth Phase Imbalances:

- ○ Challenges with change and orientation: You find it difficult to adapt to new situations or changes in your environment, often feeling disoriented when your routine is disrupted.
- ○ Excessive caregiving or controlling behavior: You may engage in overly protective or controlling behaviors, often putting the needs of others before your own to an unhealthy extent.
- ○ Indecision and uncertainty: You frequently struggle to make decisions, feeling uncertain even when faced with relatively simple choices.
- ○ Self-identity and autonomy issues: You have difficulties maintaining a strong sense of self and often rely on others for validation or direction.
- ○ Focus and thought organization difficulties: You find it challenging to maintain focus or organize your thoughts effectively, which can interfere with completing tasks.
- ○ Dependency and pleasing behavior: You tend to depend too much on others for emotional support or approval and often act primarily to please others at your own expense.
- ○ Unstable thought and decision-making processes: Your thoughts and decisions may frequently change, lacking consistency and often appear erratic or poorly planned.
- ○ Emotional dependence and exaggerated affection: You exhibit a strong emotional attachment to others, often showing affection to an excessive degree that might not be reciprocated or appropriate.
- ○ Inability to progress or stabilize: You often feel stuck, unable to move forward or find stability in various aspects of your life, from relationships to career.
- ○ Interference in personal affairs: You may intrude into the personal matters of others, offering unsolicited advice or assistance, and overstepping boundaries.

- ○ Low energy and depressive states: You frequently experience periods of low energy and feelings of sadness or hopelessness that affect your daily functioning.

- ○ Invasion of personal space and boundaries: You might struggle with respecting the personal space and boundaries of others, often invading their physical or emotional space unintentionally.

- ○ Excessive worrying and conformity: You tend to worry excessively about various aspects of life and may conform to others' expectations or societal norms without true alignment with your own desires or beliefs.

Score:

Remember, any of the imbalances you checked are simply your body's way of communicating with you that something is out of alignment. The exercises for this phase will help to restore alignment by releasing what might be causing your energy to stagnate as well as providing nourishment in areas where you've possibly depleted your energetic reserves.

Now you're ready to begin with your first exercise. The way you approach the next pages is completely up to you. However, the chart below will give you a recommendation based off your burnout level score.

- **Stages 1-2**: Follow the structured plan in the book, introducing one new exercise per week.

- **Stages 3-4**: Move to a new exercise only if you have the capacity. Otherwise, repeat the prior exercise or take a pause to rest.

- **Stage 5**: Focus only on the first exercise of the phase. Reflect deeply and discuss your experience with a mental health practitioner.

February

Weeks 1 + 3

For this month, your breathwork practice for weeks 1 and 3 will be the same. That way you can really focus on the benefits of the practice rather than losing valuable time trying to learn new mechanics of another exercise.

This breathwork is designed with the intention to vibrate and release stagnation in the Spleen and Stomach Meridian that are associated with the Earth Phase. It will also work with an energy center that we call the Yellow Court that is located right in the center below the rib cage close to the Small Intestine.

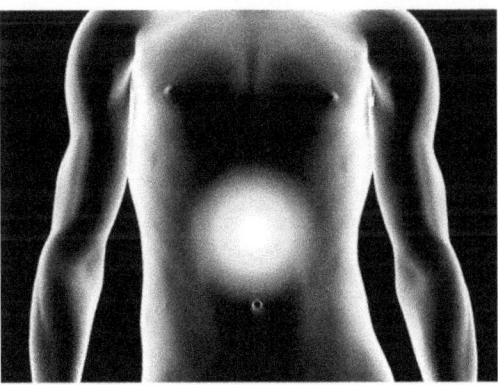

This energy center works to sort through your experiences and emotions that you aren't sure what to do with. For those experiencing burnout, I have found in my work that this energy center is often overflowing with stagnant energy. Our goal with this breathwork will be to generate movement in this center and the other two organs and their channels.

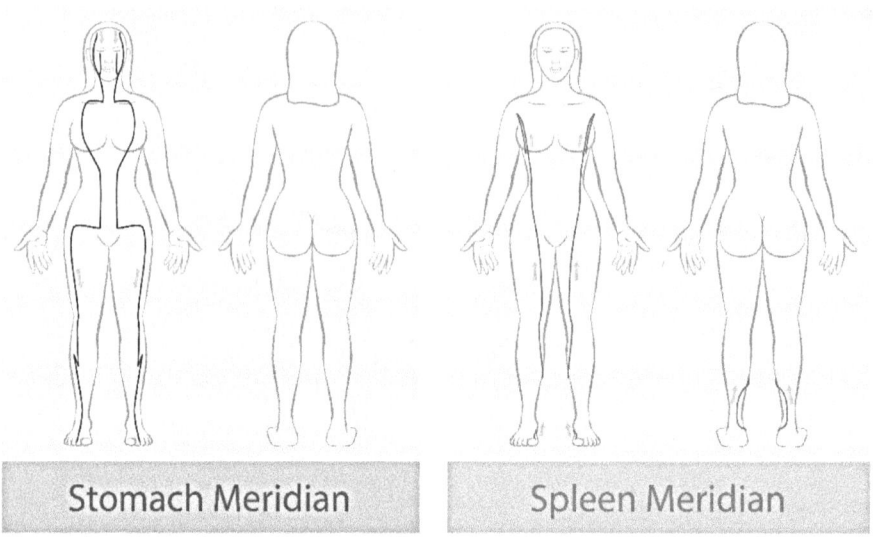

Stomach Meridian　　Spleen Meridian

This movement is critical at this time of year because stagnated energy generated as a result of the Yin time can be filled with fear that generates doubt within yourself. This is the period of time when reflection can materialize as self-sabotaging behaviors.

I highly recommend that you complete this exercise daily and even continue it on the even-numbered weeks while doing the reflective prompts. After your breathwork practice, make sure to journal and log anything that surfaced or things that you experienced. If you'd prefer to practice this exercise through a guided audio, I've created one for you. You can access it at: **www.HRartInstitute.com**.

1. Begin by focusing on your breath, tuning into your natural rhythm of the inhale and exhale.

2. Continue with your natural breathing rhythm, but guide your inhale down to the belly. When you exhale, empty the belly. Continue this pattern until it is comfortable. It is not necessary to attempt to deepen or elongate the breathing rhythm. You may do so if this happens naturally as the body relaxes, otherwise, stay with the rhythm that is comfortable for you. At no time, should you feel like you are without an adequate amount of breath.

3. Begin incorporating a visual with your inhale. Imagine that the breath is now a golden yellow mist that you inhale into your body.

Send this golden yellow mist into your Spleen and Stomach. Send this golden yellow mist and overflow your Yellow Court.

4. Now start exhaling out through the mouth while hearing in your mind or audibly making a *Hooo* sound. Imagine this sound vibrating the Spleen, Stomach, and Yellow Court, releasing stagnated emotional and mental energies. See these energies being carried out of the body by the breath on the exhale.

5. Complete 8 repetitions of inhaling the color and exhaling the sound audibly or inaudibly.

Week 2

This week, we are going to look at how that fear from the Water Phase may be attempting to materialize. This prompt will still have a very Yin feel to it, meaning that what bubbles up to the surface could feel dark, dense, and scary.

Get your journal and free-write for the following prompt for no longer than 4 minutes. Make sure you at least linger for 2 minutes before saying you're done. Please use a timer for these recommended time frames. They ensure that you give the reflection a fair shake while also not falling into a potential downward spiral. You also are encouraged to revisit this prompt each day this week, so you'll have plenty of time collectively to get out whatever may be surfacing.

Journal Prompt:

When you think of the coming year, what are you afraid might be revealed as being true about you and who you are?

Week 4

For this week's reflection, you will have an option each day to pick from one of the three prompts below. Do not attempt to answer all three every day, since Spring is right around the corner and the Yin aspect of your work is settling.

My recommendation is to answer the prompt that resonates most with you or that you actually have a response for. This might mean that you answer the same prompt every day and that is okay. It might also mean you have no responses, and nothing resonates; that's okay, too. In this case, I ask that you at least set a timer for 2 minutes and try to answer one prompt by writing down anything that comes to mind—even if what comes up is, "I don't know" or "this is dumb" or "I don't have an imbalance here." If you find that you are struggling to answer these prompts, you can choose to only engage in this practice three times this week. This will give you an opportunity to at least attempt to answer all three prompts.

Journal Prompts:

1. Who are you jealous of? Is there an individual you believe has things or a set of circumstances that you're entitled to? What do they have that you want?

2. Who are you frustrated with? Is there an individual who is currently driving you up the wall? If every little thing is like nails on a chalkboard, why do you think that is?

3. Who are you angry with? Is there an individual or group of people who have violated your boundaries? Regardless of whether you've set or held boundaries, at the core these individuals have done things that tell you they don't care about you or that they care more about themselves.

Check-In

Before moving on, let's take a minute to check on your physical and energetic Earth Phase Imbalances. This is not an evaluation of how you did during the last month, but rather a pulse check to acknowledge and know for your future work.

For each symptom listed, check the box if the symptom is present now or if you've encountered it within the past two weeks.

Potential Physical Earth Phase Imbalances:

- ○ Muscular and lymphatic dysfunction
- ○ Venous disorders
- ○ Digestive and appetite issues
- ○ Weight management difficulties
- ○ Fluid and secretion management issues
- ○ Tissue swelling and gland issues
- ○ General discomfort and pain
- ○ Reproductive and abdominal dysfunctions
- ○ Blood and vascular health issues
- ○ Eye and oral health issues
- ○ Swelling of internal organs

Score:

Potential Energetic Earth Phase Imbalances:

- ○ Challenges with change and orientation: You find it difficult to adapt to new situations or changes in your environment, often feeling disoriented when your routine is disrupted.

- ○ Excessive caregiving or controlling behavior: You may engage in overly protective or controlling behaviors, often putting the needs of others before your own to an unhealthy extent.
- ○ Indecision and uncertainty: You frequently struggle to make decisions, feeling uncertain even when faced with relatively simple choices.
- ○ Self-identity and autonomy issues: You have difficulties maintaining a strong sense of self and often rely on others for validation or direction.
- ○ Focus and thought organization difficulties: You find it challenging to maintain focus or organize your thoughts effectively, which can interfere with completing tasks.
- ○ Dependency and pleasing behavior: You tend to depend too much on others for emotional support or approval and often act primarily to please others at your own expense.
- ○ Unstable thought and decision-making processes: Your thoughts and decisions may frequently change, lacking consistency and often appear erratic or poorly planned.
- ○ Emotional dependence and exaggerated affection: You exhibit a strong emotional attachment to others, often showing affection to an excessive degree that might not be reciprocated or appropriate.
- ○ Inability to progress or stabilize: You often feel stuck, unable to move forward or find stability in various aspects of your life, from relationships to career.
- ○ Interference in personal affairs: You may intrude into the personal matters of others, offering unsolicited advice or assistance, and overstepping boundaries.
- ○ Low energy and depressive states: You frequently experience periods of low energy and feelings of sadness or hopelessness that affect your daily functioning.
- ○ Invasion of personal space and boundaries: You might struggle with respecting the personal space and boundaries of others, often invading their physical or emotional space unintentionally.

○ Excessive worrying and conformity: You tend to worry excessively about various aspects of life and may conform to others' expectations or societal norms without true alignment with your own desires or beliefs.

Score:

HONOR YOUR NEED FOR STILLNESS.

WHAT'S NEXT?

What's Next

If you've been through the seasonal exercises one full round, it is likely you realize that your healing is not done. I used to believe that the healing work is never done, however recently I've begun learning and working with the Spiritual Activator, Oliver Nino. He teaches that healing is a phase, and that really resonates with me—especially when we move toward a space and lifestyle that embraces balance and flow.

Therefore, your time in this book represents an evolution in your healing, a step forward and there isn't an infinite set of steps ahead. Each step moves you closer to yourself. A return to your purest form before life delivered stimulus that caused energetic stagnations or deviations. Yet, this journey is more than healing, its growth. Each step equips you with tools that you've learned about yourself that will allow you to sustain that peace once it's achieved. You'll know how to navigate future life events, allowing energy to carry you and work with and for you, rather than against. You'll organically be releasing and trusting, rather than suppressing and avoiding.

I say all this because, I want to invite you to consider moving through the seasons again, using them more as a framework this time. Give yourself permission to flex between your needs of continued healing and growth. Allow yourself to fill each season with practices that call to you while still honoring the intention and elemental focus. This will instill a way forward that consistently invites balance and raises your energetic vibration. This is the time to take what you've absorbed and fly, expanding your wings and enjoy this time celebrating all the changes you've gone through and loving this person you've become.

Who Have I Become

Before you begin your next step, let's spend some time taking stock of where you are in this moment. We started, with an in-depth dive of who you were and now it's important to take a moment and fully recognize and acknowledge who you've become.

To begin this taking stock process, I want to invite you to revisit your journal entries from the last year. Read without judgement instead, approach it with curiosity. Listening to what's being said and shared, acknowledging every thought and feeling with respect. Paying special attention to themes that reoccur or words that seem louder or excessively repetitive, like um distractions during a presentation. After reading these entries, take some time to free-write on the following prompts:

1. What worked well for you this year? What practices did you engage with that made you feel good?

2. What was challenging this year? When or what caused you to feel like the ask was too hard at the time?

3. How far have you come in this year? Where do you know you've grown, changed or evolved?

A Minute of Gratitude

After completing the third prompt recognizing your growth to this point, re-read it and tune inward to see if you can notice the physical vibration and frequence of gratitude as it materializes in your body. Where do you feel it? Focus on making the vibration stronger, giving it permission to grow and fill you throughout. Allow yourself to sit in this vibration for at least a full minute.

Gratitude is a powerful frequency; it is grounding and healing at the same time. Practice sitting in this frequency frequently, so that you can easily identify its presence throughout your day. You will find this frequency materializes for seconds at a time, often at moments that feel completely random. See if you can embrace these moments, being able to pause and invite that vibration to grow and fill you up. It's an incredible way to maintain connection with the energetic foundation you've been working hard to establish.

Let's End with How We Began

It's time now to end, the same way we started, by establishing your new baseline. Complete the Burnout Assessment below and create your new Core Map by returning to Chapter 7. Remember the goal of revisiting both of these exercises are to increase awareness about your current state, so try your best to push judgment aside. Use your outcomes from these two exercises to serve as the foundation for your next evolution of growth.

REST IS A DECISION, NOT AN INDULGENCE.

Burnout Re-assessment

A few reminders about this assessment:

- This assessment includes a list of physical and psychological symptoms. Some of the symptoms might feel a bit strange given the fact that we are talking about burnout, which has been ingrained in us to associate strictly with the professional environment. I'm going to invite you to open your mind, letting go of that separation, and instead see it as a whole and connected to your overall well-being. Plus, keep in mind that you are the only one who is going to see your answers. For this work, your honesty with yourself, without any judgment, will be key to cultivating the healing you most need right now.

- This assessment is also quite extensive. My recommendation would be to complete one section per day, to ensure you do not get assessment fatigue that will ultimately hinder your results. With that being said, the assessment is structured in a fashion that inquires about the most pressing symptoms in relation to burnout first.

- When it comes to scoring, each section has specific directions on how to calculate your totals to generate your results. However, there is one rule that is consistent throughout this assessment. If you check fewer than three boxes in a section, the score for that section is automatically zero.

Let's begin.

Physical Water Phase Imbalances

For each symptom listed, check the box if the symptom is present now or if you've encountered it within the past year.

- ○ Memory problems and trouble focusing
- ○ Difficulties with movement and sensing changes
- ○ Alterations in bone, joint, and dental health
- ○ Issues with physical development and reproductive health
- ○ Problems with managing body fluids
- ○ Cysts, swelling, or hardening in reproductive and urinary organs
- ○ Irregular sleep patterns, including trouble waking up
- ○ Vision and hearing problems
- ○ Ringing in the ears (tinnitus)
- ○ Weakness and stiffness in the body and joints
- ○ Wear and tear on spinal disks and cartilage
- ○ Cold feelings in the lower body
- ○ Need to urinate more often
- ○ Bone thinning (osteoporosis)
- ○ Early signs of aging (gray hair, hair loss, wrinkles)
- ○ Fertility issues or sexual health problems
- ○ Fatigue or low energy levels
- ○ Reduced appetite
- ○ Weakness in abdominal muscles
- ○ Changes in skin color or texture
- ○ Headaches, especially around the eyes or top of the head
- ○ Decreased sweating and less frequent urination
- ○ Stiffening of blood vessels and cartilage
- ○ Kidney or bladder stones
- ○ Development of bony growths
- ○ Digestive issues

- ○ Receding gums (gum health problems)
- ○ Sleeping less than usual
- ○ Constipation or trouble with bowel movements
- ○ High blood pressure (hypertension)

Scoring for Section:

1. **Count the Symptoms**: If the total number of symptoms is less than 3, record a score of zero. If the total is 3 or more, note the total as the "Water Physical Phase Imbalance Score."
2. **Determine Burnout Level**: Take the "Water Physical Phase Imbalance Score" and multiply it by three. Add the result to the corresponding open slot in the tally table to determine the overall burnout level.

Total Score:

Energetic Water Phase Imbalances

For each symptom listed, check the box if the symptom is present now or if you've encountered it within the past year.

- ○ Social interaction challenges: You may find it difficult to engage in social activities or feel uncomfortable during social interactions.
- ○ Communication difficulties: You might struggle to clearly express your thoughts and feelings to others.
- ○ Discomfort in social exposure: You could feel uneasy or anxious when you are the center of attention or in large groups.
- ○ Critical behavior: You often find yourself criticizing others or focusing on their faults
- ○ Negative worldview: You tend to see the world in a negative light and often expect the worst outcomes.
- ○ Health anxiety: You frequently worry about your health and may be preoccupied with fears of becoming ill.
- ○ Immobility episodes: There are times when you feel so overwhelmed that you become physically immobile or emotionally unresponsive.
- ○ Observational preference: You prefer to watch others rather than participate in activities directly.
- ○ Imaginative thought processes: Your thinking often involves fantasy or unrealistic scenarios.
- ○ Financial frugality: You are extremely cautious about spending money, often to the point of avoiding necessary expenses.
- ○ Distracted by thoughts: You frequently find your mind wandering, and you have trouble focusing on the task at hand.
- ○ Intense observation: You tend to observe people and situations very closely, often noticing details that others miss.
- ○ Aloofness: You generally keep your distance from others and might come off as detached or uninterested.
- ○ Behavioral analysis: You often analyze people's behavior, trying to understand their motives and actions.

- ○ Unconventional behavior: Your behavior or thinking often deviates from the norm, and you are not afraid to be different.
- ○ Suspicion and covetousness: You may be overly suspicious of others' motives or envious of their achievements and possessions.

Scoring for Section:

3. **Count the Symptoms**: If the total number of symptoms is less than 3, record a score of zero. If the total is 3 or more, note the total as the "Water Phase Energetic Imbalance Score."

4. **Determine Burnout Level**: Take the "Water Phase Energetic Imbalance Score" and multiply it by two. Add the result to the corresponding open slot in the tally table to determine the overall burnout level.

Total Score:

Physical Wood Phase Imbalances

For each symptom listed, check the box if the symptom is present now or if you've encountered it within the past year.

- ○ Hypertension (including labile blood pressure)
- ○ Oily skin/hair
- ○ Boils
- ○ Muscle cramps in limbs
- ○ Vertigo
- ○ Hearing issues (including ringing in ears)
- ○ Spasmodic constipation
- ○ Sciatic pain
- ○ Pain in ribs
- ○ Heartburn
- ○ Swallowing difficulties
- ○ Eye and ear pain
- ○ Shingles
- ○ Increased clumsiness and susceptibility to accidents
- ○ Nail conditions (including dry, brittle, and thick nails)
- ○ Breast pain
- ○ Tendon conditions (including injuries and tendonitis)
- ○ Hypoglycemia
- ○ Blurry vision
- ○ Sensitivity to light and sound
- ○ Urinary tract issues (including cystitis, urethritis)
- ○ Itchiness in eyes and genital/anal areas
- ○ Joint and muscle conditions (including lax joints and tense muscles)
- ○ Irritable bowel syndrome
- ○ Chronic neck and shoulder tension
- ○ Headaches (including occipital and lateral)

- ○ Migraines
- ○ Jaw joint dysfunction (TMJ syndrome)
- ○ Facial nerve pain
- ○ Peripheral neuropathy
- ○ Sexual dysfunction
- ○ Menstrual issues (including painful cycles and PMS)
- ○ Substance abuse

Scoring for Section:

3. **Count the Symptoms**: If the total number of symptoms is less than 3, record a score of zero. If the total is 3 or more, note the total as the "Wood Phase Physical Imbalance Score."

4. **Determine Burnout Level**: Take the "Wood Phase Physical Imbalance Score" and multiply it by two. Add the result to the corresponding open slot in the tally table to determine the overall burnout level.

Total Score:

Energetic Wood Phase Imbalances

For each symptom listed, check the box if the symptom is present now or if you've encountered it within the past year.

- ○ Intense and forceful behavior: You often exhibit behavior that is aggressive or overly assertive, which can be overwhelming to others.
- ○ Lack of restraint: You find it difficult to control your impulses or refrain from acting on your immediate desires.
- ○ Difficulty in fair interactions: You struggle to engage in interactions that require fairness and equity, often prioritizing your own needs or views.
- ○ Challenges in collaboration: Working with others is difficult for you, especially when it involves compromising or sharing responsibilities.
- ○ Discomfort with uncertainty: You feel uneasy or anxious in situations where outcomes are uncertain or unknown.
- ○ Hostile behavior: You may frequently behave in a hostile manner, which can include being verbally or physically confrontational.
- ○ Overbearing attitudes: Your demeanor can be excessively controlling or demanding, often trying to impose your will on others.
- ○ Unpredictable or poorly considered actions: You tend to act without thinking things through, leading to unpredictable or rash decisions.
- ○ Inconsistent decision-making: Your decision-making process often lacks consistency, changing based on mood or external pressures.
- ○ Oppositional behavior: You regularly exhibit resistance or opposition in situations where cooperation is expected.
- ○ Domineering interactions: In your interactions with others, you tend to dominate the conversation or situation, often at the expense of others' participation.
- ○ Easily irritated behavior: You are quick to become irritated or annoyed, often over seemingly minor issues.

Scoring for Section:

3. **Count the Symptoms**: If the total number of symptoms is less than 3, record a score of zero. If the total is 3 or more, note the total as the "Wood Phase Energetic Imbalance Score."

4. **Determine Burnout Level**: Take the "Wood Phase Energetic Imbalance Score" and add the result to the corresponding open slot in the tally table to determine the overall burnout level. Recognize that this is the only phase that does not have a multiplier, this was intentional in the design.

Total Score:

Physical Fire Phase Imbalances

For each symptom listed, check the box if the symptom is present now or if you've encountered it within the past year.

- ○ Sleep disturbances
- ○ Heart conditions
- ○ Irregular heart functions
- ○ Circulatory system disorders
- ○ Facial complexion changes
- ○ Heat regulation issues
- ○ Sexual response issues
- ○ Skin conditions
- ○ Pulmonary hypertension
- ○ Painful urination
- ○ Anemia
- ○ Speech and sensation disturbances
- ○ Chest pain

Scoring for Section:

3. **Count the Symptoms**: If the total number of symptoms is less than 3, record a score of zero. If the total is 3 or more, note the total as the "Fire Phase Physical Imbalance Score."

4. **Determine Burnout Level**: Take the "Fire Phase Physical Imbalance Score" and multiply it by two. Add the result to the corresponding open slot in the tally table to determine the overall burnout level.

Total Score:

Energetic Fire Phase Imbalances

For each symptom listed, check the box if the symptom is present now or if you've encountered it within the past year.

- ○ Boundary issues: You often have difficulty setting and maintaining personal boundaries, which might lead to feeling overwhelmed or taken advantage of by others.
- ○ Pacing and stimulation management: You find it challenging to manage and maintain a comfortable pace in activities, often feeling either overstimulated or understimulated.
- ○ Anxiety about the unknown: You experience significant anxiety when faced with uncertain situations or future outcomes that are not clear.
- ○ Sleep disturbances: You frequently have trouble either falling asleep or staying asleep, which impacts your overall health and well-being.
- ○ Expression difficulties: You struggle to clearly express your thoughts and feelings, which can lead to misunderstandings or a sense of isolation.
- ○ Heightened startle response: You are easily startled by unexpected sounds or movements, more so than others.
- ○ Cognitive imbalances: You experience difficulties in your thought processes, which can manifest as disorganized thinking or difficulty concentrating.
- ○ Hypersensitivity: You are extremely sensitive to physical sensations, emotions, or social interactions, often feeling overwhelmed by them.
- ○ Social flirtation and seduction: You tend to engage frequently in flirtatious or seductive behavior, which may affect your social interactions.
- ○ Elevated emotional responses: Your emotional reactions are often more intense than the situation warrants, which can be draining for you and those around you.

- ○ Overly positive outlook: You maintain an excessively optimistic view, even in situations where such optimism may not be warranted.
- ○ Intense emotional feelings toward others: You often feel deep and overwhelming emotions toward others, which can affect your personal relationships.
- ○ Difficulty with emotional or physical detachment: You find it hard to detach yourself from situations or relationships, even when they are harmful or unfulfilling.
- ○ Excessive talking: You tend to talk more than most people, often dominating conversations or speaking without thinking about the impact on others.
- ○ Naivety in trust: You often trust people too readily, which can lead to disappointment or exploitation.

Scoring for Section:

3. **Count the Symptoms**: If the total number of symptoms is less than 3, record a score of zero. If the total is 3 or more, note the total as the "Fire Phase Energetic Imbalance Score."
4. **Determine Burnout Level**: Take the "Fire Phase Energetic Imbalance Score" and add the result to the corresponding open slot in the tally table to determine the overall burnout level.

Total Score:

Physical Earth Phase Imbalances

For each symptom listed, check the box if the symptom is present now or if you've encountered it within the past year.

- ○ Muscular and lymphatic dysfunction
- ○ Venous disorders
- ○ Digestive and appetite issues
- ○ Weight management difficulties
- ○ Fluid and secretion management issues
- ○ Tissue swelling and gland issues
- ○ General discomfort and pain
- ○ Reproductive and abdominal dysfunctions
- ○ Blood and vascular health issues
- ○ Eye and oral health issues
- ○ Swelling of internal organs

Scoring for Section:

3. **Count the Symptoms**: If the total number of symptoms is less than 3, record a score of zero. If the total is 3 or more, note the total as the "Earth Phase Physical Imbalance Score."

4. **Determine Burnout Level**: Take the "Earth Phase Physical Imbalance Score" and multiply it by 2.5. Add the result to the corresponding open slot in the tally table to determine the overall burnout level.

Total Score:

Energetic Earth Phase Imbalances

For each symptom listed, check the box if the symptom is present now or if you've encountered it within the past year.

- ○ Challenges with change and orientation: You find it difficult to adapt to new situations or changes in your environment, often feeling disoriented when your routine is disrupted.
- ○ Excessive caregiving or controlling behavior: You may engage in overly protective or controlling behaviors, often putting the needs of others before your own to an unhealthy extent.
- ○ Indecision and uncertainty: You frequently struggle to make decisions, feeling uncertain even when faced with relatively simple choices.
- ○ Self-identity and autonomy issues: You have difficulties maintaining a strong sense of self and often rely on others for validation or direction.
- ○ Focus and thought organization difficulties: You find it challenging to maintain focus or organize your thoughts effectively, which can interfere with completing tasks.
- ○ Dependency and pleasing behavior: You tend to depend too much on others for emotional support or approval and often act primarily to please others at your own expense.
- ○ Unstable thought and decision-making processes: Your thoughts and decisions may frequently change, lacking consistency and often appear erratic or poorly planned.
- ○ Emotional dependence and exaggerated affection: You exhibit a strong emotional attachment to others, often showing affection to an excessive degree that might not be reciprocated or appropriate.
- ○ Inability to progress or stabilize: You often feel stuck, unable to move forward or find stability in various aspects of your life, from relationships to career.

- ○ Interference in personal affairs: You may intrude into the personal matters of others, offering unsolicited advice or assistance, and overstepping boundaries.
- ○ Low energy and depressive states: You frequently experience periods of low energy and feelings of sadness or hopelessness that affect your daily functioning.
- ○ Invasion of personal space and boundaries: You might struggle with respecting the personal space and boundaries of others, often invading their physical or emotional space unintentionally.
- ○ Excessive worrying and conformity: You tend to worry excessively about various aspects of life and may conform to others' expectations or societal norms without true alignment with your own desires or beliefs.

Scoring for Section:

3. **Count the Symptoms**: If the total number of symptoms is less than 3, record a score of zero. If the total is 3 or more, note the total as the "Earth Phase Energetic Imbalance Score."
4. **Determine Burnout Level**: Take the "Earth Phase Energetic Imbalance Score" and multiply it by 1.5. Add the result to the corresponding open slot in the tally table to determine the overall burnout level.

Total Score:

Physical Metal Phase Imbalances

For each symptom listed, check the box if the symptom is present now or if you've encountered it within the past year.

- ○ Respiratory issues
- ○ Skin and integumentary issues
- ○ Fluid balance and hydration issues
- ○ Elimination system dysfunctions
- ○ Circulatory system problems
- ○ Nasal and sinus conditions
- ○ Sweat-related symptoms
- ○ Musculoskeletal rigidity
- ○ Emotional trigger-related symptoms
- ○ Cardiorespiratory reflections

Scoring for Section:

3. **Count the Symptoms**: If the total number of symptoms is less than 3, record a score of zero. If the total is 3 or more, note the total as the "Metal Phase Physical Imbalance Score."

4. **Determine Burnout Level**: Take the "Metal Phase Physical Imbalance Score" and multiply it by two. Add the result to the corresponding open slot in the tally table to determine the overall burnout level.

Total Score:

Energetic Metal Phase Imbalances

Place a check next to any symptom you are currently experiencing, or have experienced in the last year.

- ○ Control and authority issues: You often struggle with situations where you need to assert control or respond to authority, which may result in conflict or discomfort.
- ○ Difficulty with emotional challenges: You find it hard to manage and respond effectively to emotional stress, often feeling overwhelmed or unable to cope.
- ○ Relationship and intimacy difficulties: You experience challenges in forming or maintaining close relationships, often due to fear of intimacy or inability to connect on a deeper level.
- ○ Rigidity in perspectives and behavior: You tend to have a fixed way of thinking and acting, finding it difficult to adapt or consider alternative viewpoints or approaches.
- ○ Need for order and perfection: You have a strong desire for everything to be in order and perfect, which can lead to frustration when things do not meet your high standards.
- ○ Formal and prescribed behaviors: You often adhere strictly to formal rules or socially prescribed behaviors, sometimes at the expense of spontaneity or personal expression.
- ○ Superficial concerns and behaviors: You may focus on surface-level issues or engage in behaviors that lack depth and genuine engagement.
- ○ Discrepancies in beliefs and actions: There is often a gap between what you believe and how you act, which can lead to internal conflict or perceptions of hypocrisy.
- ○ Emotional responsiveness issues: You may have difficulties in responding appropriately to emotional cues or situations, often appearing detached or overly emotional.

- ○ Behavioral standards and conduct: You hold yourself and others to very high standards of behavior, which can lead to judgment or dissatisfaction with people's conduct.
- ○ Elusiveness in convictions: You might show a tendency to be vague or non-committal in your beliefs and opinions, often avoiding taking a firm stance on issues.

Scoring for Section:

3. **Count the Symptoms**: If the total number of symptoms is less than 3, record a score of zero. If the total is 3 or more, note the total as the "Metal Phase Energetic Imbalance Score."
4. **Determine Burnout Level**: Take the "Metal Phase Energetic Imbalance Score" and add the result to the corresponding open slot in the tally table to determine the overall burnout level.

Total Score:

Re-assessment Results

Active Imbalance Report

Phase	Physical	Energetic	Total
Water			
Wood			
Fire			
Earth			
Metal			

Current Burnout Level

Water Phase Physical Imbalance Score **x 3**	
Water Phase Energetic Imbalance Score **x 2**	
Wood Phase Physical Imbalance Score **x 2**	
Wood Phase Energetic Imbalance Score **x 1**	
Fire Phase Physical Imbalance Score **x 2**	
Fire Phase Energetic Imbalance Score **x 1**	
Earth Phase Physical Imbalance Score **x 2.5**	
Earth Phase Energetic Imbalance Score **x 1.5**	
Metal Phase Physical Imbalance Score **x 2**	
Metal Phase Energetic Imbalance Score **x 1**	
Total	

Reference Assessment Results, page 33, to determine the meaning of your score. Once you do, I have a few final thoughts in a letter that follow for you, based on your newest results.

A Letter to Those with an Engaged Score

Congratulations on the work you've done to care for yourself energetically. You've reached a place of engagement, and this book can now serve as your perfect maintenance program. When life feels messy or overwhelming, return to these pages and revisit what resonated with you most. Let it remind you of the tools you've built to sustain your energy and balance.

You've accomplished something powerful, but sustaining it will be your greatest challenge in a world that may not see the value in the practices you've established. Be mindful of the times of year or elemental phases that felt most challenging—these are likely when you're most prone to becoming ungrounded. Knowing this will help you navigate those moments with greater ease and self-compassion.

I also have a favor to ask: You are living proof of what is possible when healing and growth are embraced. Please consider visiting and engaging **HRartInstitute.com** regularly to share your story, offer support, or provide a testimony for others in our community. Your voice matters. Your experience can inspire and uplift those who are still finding their way.

Together, we can create a ripple of healing and hope that touches more lives than we can imagine. Thank you for being part of this journey and for showing what's possible when we choose to heal.

With gratitude,

Samm

A Letter to the Stressed and Disconnected

You would deeply benefit from another journey through the seasons, gently encouraging yourself to take steps you may have previously talked yourself out of. I know time feels like your greatest obstacle—there's always something demanding your attention. But every moment we don't choose ourselves allows burnout to creep further in.

Your body is already speaking to you, trying to communicate its needs. If you don't listen, those signals will grow louder and harder to ignore. At the start of every year, many of us set intentions with hope, only to find ourselves pulled away by life's distractions. This year, I invite you to set just one intention: to honor yourself.

Pay attention when your body is trying to get your attention. When you notice that signal, turn to this book. Find the season or elemental phase that resonates with where you are and begin there. Don't worry about doing everything perfectly or completing the program in its entirety. This isn't a test, and skipping parts isn't a failure.

Instead, know that the pace you follow—whether slow, steady, or sporadic—is the rhythm your body and soul need to make this healing last. Give yourself grace. Trust that the steps you take, no matter how small, are leading you toward something greater: a lasting connection to yourself and your well-being.

You are worthy of this journey. You always have been.

With care,

Samm

A Letter to the Disengaged

A journey through the seasons may feel impossible right now—and to be honest, it probably is. What you need isn't another plan or practice. What you need is rest.

I'm asking you to take a year and choose rest above all else. Any time you'd normally set aside for self-help or healing, let it be time for simply being. Don't force a ritual, an action, or an outcome. Instead, find a quiet space where you can just exist, with no expectations. If your mind won't stop racing, that's okay. Let the thoughts come and go, but remind yourself that for the next 20 minutes, you will not act on them.

One day, without you forcing it, your mind will begin to slow. It may not become silent, but it will become intentional. Thoughts and feelings will shift from pressure to flow. This is the beginning of the healing you are seeking.

For now, your only job is to just *be*. Find time to sit with yourself, free from internal or external expectations of what should happen. It's in this space—this quiet permission to exist as you are—that true healing and recovery will start.

With compassion,

Samm

A Letter to the Burned Out

The most important thing I need you to hear is this: You are not alone. What you are experiencing is the result of years of putting others before yourself. Burnout is your body's desperate call to choose you, to find you, and to be you.

Please don't try to do this alone. Reach out and find the support you need. Start by connecting with a mental health professional you trust—someone who can help you create a safe space to gently peel back the layers of what has been suppressed, avoided, or buried. This is where healing begins.

Also, meet with your Primary Care Provider to discuss ways to make each day more manageable as you embark on this journey. This may include advocating for yourself by considering options like a leave of absence if your work environment is making healing impossible. Choosing yourself is not selfish—it's necessary.

Burnout can feel isolating, overwhelming, and endless, but it's also a signal. It's your body's way of asking you to prioritize your own well-being. I see you, and I believe in your capacity to heal. You don't have to do this perfectly; you just have to take the first step.

With care,

Samm

Acknowledgments

To my editor and publisher, Demi Stevens, and Year of the Book Press: Once again, this is all possible because of you. You hold me accountable, help me get the words on the page, and breathe life into the writer within me. Thank you for believing in my voice and guiding me every step of the way.

To the amazing Beta Book Club members: Your openness, vulnerability, and thoughtful feedback shaped this book into the powerful tool it has become. Thank you for trusting the process and for sharing your journeys with me.

To my incredible HRart family: Your unwavering support and belief in me have been the foundation of this work. You inspire me to keep going and remind me of the greater purpose behind it all.

To my girls, Maddy and Zoey: You are the future and my greatest teachers. Thank you for ensuring I see the world through fresh eyes every day. You remind me to stay curious, creative, and hopeful.

And to my husband, Josh, the love of my life: You always believed in me, even when I struggled to believe in myself. You carried me when the world felt too heavy, and you never let me give up. I stand here today because of you. I love you more than words can ever express.

Thank you all for being part of this journey. This book exists because of you.

About the Author

Samm Smeltzer believes that HR Professionals have the answers to our workplace's greatest challenges. After a 10 year career as a multi-award-winning HR Practitioner, Samm has spent the last decade as CEO of her own company, The HRart ("heart") Center, where she works with leadership teams to create cultural shifts that are focused on restoring humanity in the workplace which increases retention and engagement. With a doctorate in Medical Qigong ("chee-gong"), Samm brings both Western and Eastern perspectives on wellness into workplaces to heal burnout and disengagement.

Author of four books, her most recent, Workplace Healers, builds the case that HR should be more than just the compliance department, and puts forward her ideas on how allowing HR professionals to take care of their own energy is key to building thriving workplaces.

www.ingramcontent.com/pod-product-compliance
Lightning Source LLC
Chambersburg PA
CBHW042351070526
44585CB00028B/2894